ASK AN INDIAN
ABOUT INDIA

ASK AN

INDIAN ABOUT INDIA

BLAISE LEVAI

Friendship Press—New York

CONTENTS

Library of Congress Catalog Card No.: 71-182980

Copyright © 1972 by Friendship Press, Inc.
Printed in the United States of America

*I would like you to think of this major ad-
venture of India that is taking place today.
Criticize it whenever there is any failure,
whenever there is any falling off,
whenever there is weakness.
Criticism will be an incentive to better
work.
But try to understand and appreciate
that something magnificent and co-
lossal is happening in India.*

—Jawaharlal Nehru

FOREWORD

I believe *Ask an Indian about India* will prove to be an outstanding presentation to the American as well as the Indian public emphasizing the life, problems, achievements, struggles and also the rather quiet assets of the peoples of India.

The book is a fascinating collection of conversations with individual Indians ranging from the prime minister to peasants. But there are interviews and interviews. Some bring out more the views of the interviewer than his or her subject. Such egocentricity is absent from Dr. Blaise Levai's book. He focuses exclusively on his subjects and presents India unvarnished, genuine and without the biases of any one author, foreign or indigenous.

The reader will find a refreshing variety of Indian views and opinions such as, for example, a defense of the Indian variety of socialism (which is a pragmatic nondogmatic brand) and a vigorous plea for unadulterated capitalism. He will realize from the words of Indians themselves how free expression is in that vast society. In India there are more people than the total population of the thirty or more countries of the Caribbean, North, Central and South America. The human freedoms in India appear to be well grounded, in spite of the fact that around India for the most part much more severely restrictive regimes hold sway. India's problems should be of special concern to all democratic countries.

Then again, the drama of modern India which comes across so powerfully in this book has another current world relevance. India contains a melange of peoples ranging from the Nordic Aryans and the Scythian Goths to the pre-Aryan southern inhabitants, and from Mongolians to Semites. In religion and culture, too, the Indian scene is richly variegated.

A significant aspect of the long-continuing Indian experiment is an attempt to achieve a synthesis that permits, and indeed encourages, the tolerant and mutually enriching cooperation of a large variety of peoples. The United States is in the throes of a comparable experiment; and this is, after all, the kind of experiment upon which the whole of our small world must vigorously embark if respect for life and a peaceful commingling of peoples are to triumph over conflicts producing divisions and dogmatisms. This book may well contribute to lighting the way.

ARTHUR LALL *Former Ambassador from India to the USA and Permanent Representative to the United Nations*

INTRODUCTION

This book includes conversations with Indians from many parts of the country, representing varied professions—medical-scientific, educational, religious, cultural—and family relationships.

These contemporary views should help the reader see the struggles and the development going on in India today. One of the most populated independent nations in Asia, it represents one-sixth of the world's population.

The book takes an inside look at the potentialities of people in an ancient land to help the reader better understand the aspirations of people of a different language, culture and religion. It is not easy to survey the vast changes taking place in India. So heterogeneous are the influences at work—the tensions and frustrations of the human revolution—that no one volume can comprehensively analyze modern India. In view of the limited number of pages in this book, border tensions with Pakistan and China are necessarily omitted.

These different points of view, drawing upon the insights and findings of outstanding Indians, can, however, provide an intensive look at India as it really is today.

It is hoped that these views will stimulate the Christian church to care, and to take whatever steps are necessary to face up to the accelerating changes taking place in one of the most important free nations in Asia. Surely understanding and anticipating the dynamics of change, whether we live in India or America, is crucial to our survival. And the struggle of the peoples of India for nationalism, self-respect and an equitable economic system may affect the lives of human beings for generations to come.

Blaise Levai

india at a glance

1. Population: over 550 million; second most populous country in the world
2. Largest democracy in the world; one-third of the people of the underdeveloped free world
3. Present population will double to more than one billion by year 2000
4. Two percent of population is Christian
5. One out of every six people in the world is an Indian
6. Area: one million square miles; over 500 people per square mile
7. Nation's highest birth rate recorded in Central India; lowest in South India.
8. Highest death rate in Central India; lowest in North India
9. Languages and dialects: 875; main languages: 15
10. Average life expectancy: 41 years
11. About 70 percent illiterate
12. Some portion of the Bible has been translated into 105 languages

13. There is one portion of Scripture for every 300 literates
14. Eighty-three percent of the Indian people live in villages
15. Agriculture provides livelihood for 70 percent of the people and accounts for nearly half the total income
16. Per capita income: about $76—a 6.2 percent increase over 1968
17. One million people die each year from malaria and tuberculosis
18. There is one physician for every five thousand people
19. There is one nurse for every seven thousand people
20. India has one-fourth of world's total cattle, but average yield per annum is only 413 pounds of milk—the lowest in the world
21. The Indian film industry is the second largest in the world
22. The Indian railway system is the largest in Asia and fourth largest in the world

INDIAN GOVERNMENT —

india puts democratic socialism
to the test

Indira Gandhi

What are your hopes and aspirations for India?

These remarks are naturally affected by the current political scene. Whether I am prime minister or not, these are my aspirations for India. I do not mind if I am not in power. But I do want my progressive policies to be carried out so that India can keep pace with the developing countries.

Despite many pitfalls and difficulties, India is on the march. India's democracy has survived many crises—both internal and external—since her struggle for independence. The people of India face other crucial tests. They have to choose cautiously between progress and stagnation, stability and confusion, unity and disruption.

The country today needs a strong central government under united and homogeneous leadership, firmly committed to progressive policies for elimination of poverty and all-round advancement of the entire nation.

Local problems must be subordinated to large issues facing our entire nation. If at an important juncture such as this, continued stress is given to local problems, then in the process major national and international issues would be sidetracked, much to India's detriment.

India is on a long and difficult pilgrimage. There are no short-cuts.

Mrs. Gandhi was reelected Prime Minister on March 10, 1971, by an overwhelming two-thirds majority.

OLICIES & PROBLEMS

We are a democracy. We have to persuade people rather than compel them. We have to bring about a change in the outlook of people through education and persuasion.

—*Indira Gandhi*

We have taken our first step and achieved independence from the British. This was done with the full and active participation of our people. Our nation must not stop here. Now we must uncompromisingly launch upon a progressive program to remove poverty. Since our freedom struggle, significant progress has been achieved in varied fields of industry, agriculture and education. But despite this progress many problems still await solution. Millions live in poverty in villages and countryside. Justice—social, economic and political—the basis of our constitution, is yet a goal to be fought for and attained. Our people are rightly impatient in their ardent desire for a speedier and more resolute advance towards this goal.

Many areas still remain backward and the fruits of freedom have not yet reached our people who suffer. As long as these conditions of social and economic inequality continue, peace in society will be endangered. For this reason, India has taken the decisive path of socialism to break through barriers of the *haves* and *have-nots.*

Overpopulation, underdevelopment, unemployment, hunger, rising prices, social disparity and violence in parts of India are problems facing India today. But these problems are found not only in India; they exist all over the world. Because the people in India are so very poor, the burden of these new and age-old problems is heavier. Specific steps are being taken to remove inequality which in turn can diminish poverty and provide equal opportunity to all people. Poverty should not be a handicap to so many.

What steps have been taken to solve these problems?

Practical steps now being taken are in the right direction. While results are admittedly small, these steps must be implemented vigorously. Some extremists and reactionary forces have taken to violence to solve these problems. By pursuing a middle of the road policy, necessary change is being initiated through peaceful democratic means. The intention is not to unjustly take away anything from anyone, but to help the exploited poor. The question of being inimically disposed towards any groups or individuals does not arise at all in achieving progress.

Trust is essential. Our people should view these problems from the nation's angle and in trust help establish a strong and stable government at the center to enable the country to move ahead in its pilgrimage of banishing poverty and unemployment. Once the government takes positive steps pursuing right policies, not only India and her people would prosper but many local problems of the state could be solved. Trust involves risks. A unified India depends upon unified people. Irrational, violent methods will not solve any problems. Violent activities in West Bengal, for example (by the Naxalites), have led to disastrous consequences. India faces a brighter future by peacefully dealing with these problems through democratic socialism.

Is socialism the only way?

My father, Jawaharlal Nehru, believed India was committed to socialism. I deny the charge that I am taking the country towards Russia. Such criticism was even leveled against my father when he was prime minister. Therefore, I do not attach any importance to it.

Our democratic socialism is not copied from any other socialist system. Our socialistic goal has arisen from our own historical experience and it can solve many of the problems faced by our nation. Our democratic system of government should suit the conditions prevailing here. This is imperative in order to avoid problems faced by certain other countries. Socialism is a means to an end. My basic objective is a new India—a new person and a new civilization in which India can fulfill her role in present world activities. Such a civilization cannot flourish on poverty, inequality, tyranny and totalitarianism.

Even before independence in 1947, it was agreed that socialism was the only way for a poverty-stricken nation. Some prominent personalities oppose this form of government. Why? Perhaps because they are afraid of socialism. There are other individuals who believed in socialism, but now disavow it because they want to achieve quick results through violence. But violence ultimately sets the clock back.

Even prior to independence the path of democracy was chosen so that our people could select their leaders and decide policies. And such a selection requires deep thought and the careful consideration of responsible men, women and youth. India's future depends upon her youth.

Through this democratic process—social, political and economic —freedom must now become meaningful for the masses of our people. The cooperation of people, in spite of differences, is essen-

tial. Every Indian must be willing to shed age-old lethargy, resig-
nation and contentment with the status quo. We must realize the
aspirations of Gandhi and Nehru and then go on to a new stage
of development. As Indians we cannot keep looking back all the
time. We have to face new challenges and create new eras while
guided by the values, ideals and sacrifices of those who fought and
won the struggle for our independence.

the role of government in providing total health facilities

S. Chandrasekhar

What is India's health objective?

The First Five-Year Plan has defined health with special refer-
ence to conditions in India:

Health is a positive state of well-being in which the harmonious development of physical and mental capacities of the individual lead to
the enjoyment of a rich and full life. It is not a negative state of mere
absence of disease. Health further implies primarily the application of
social science for the benefit of the individual and society. But many
other factors—social, economic and educational—have an intimate bear-
ing on the health of a community. Health is thus a vital part of a
concurrent and integrated program of development of all aspects of community life.

Before one can think of achieving health for a community one
must analyze the factors and forces responsible for the nation's
current morbidity and mortality.

Unfortunately, our morbidity and mortality statistics, by age,
sex and cause, are scanty. But we can judge from the available
evidence that probably about a third of the total sickness in the
country is traceable to bad drinking water.

Therefore, it is simple common sense that if good drinking water

Dr. Chandrasekhar is the former Union Minister of State for Health and Family Planning, New Delhi.

Based on an address by S. Chandrasekhar, *Prevention Is Better Than Cure.*
New Delhi: Central Family Planning Institute, 1970. Used by permission.

is made available in every community—and we hope eventually in every home—no matter what the size of the hamlet or village, about a third of the total sickness will disappear. At the least, if we can educate the average citizen—the villager and the small town dweller—to filter and boil drinking water and to protect all food and drink from contamination of flies and dust, an incredible number of cases of dysentery, gastroenteritis, enteric fever and chronic amoebiasis will disappear. Such a simple preventive approach will not only eliminate unnecessary suffering but save on doctors' services, hospital beds and drugs, granting that a segment of those who suffer now obtain some medical care.

What is the primary cause of sickness and death in India today?

Roughly a third of all sickness and death is probably caused directly or indirectly by our extremely poor and depressing sanitation and public hygiene. The lack of closed or underground drainage for the disposal of domestic sewage and industrial effluent, inefficient removal and disposal of garbage, the lack of water-closet latrines, the want of consciousness regarding general public hygiene that results in spitting anywhere and committing acts of nuisance in public places and general littering—these are direct causes of sickness, suffering and death in the community.

Probably about another third of all our morbidity is the product of malnutrition and undernutrition. Actually, although it is impossible to gauge with any accuracy the effect of our widespread malnutrition on the nation's health, it is probable that it contributes to the lack of resistance to disease in far greater measure than we have been aware in the past. Any general practitioner who has spent time in the rural areas will bear witness that a third to a half of all the patients who throng to a rural health center would not need to be there if their daily diet were anywhere near an adequate level with some protein, vitamin A and iron.

Poor nutritional levels are the product of both poverty and ignorance: poverty because most families cannot afford a balanced diet or protective foods; ignorance because even those who can afford desirable diets do not consume them for want of knowledge of what a healthy diet is. But even the relatively poor families could choose a more balanced diet if they had knowledge of what is most important in one's diet, especially for children.

Protein malnutrition is a problem of disturbing dimensions, although we have only recently become fully aware of it and its implications. Protein deficiency in childhood, particularly in the preschool age, according to recent available evidence, can lead to permanent physical and possibly mental retardation, and thereby limit the productive capacity of the individual and the nation.

Better nutrition not only insures against infant and childhood mortality and promotes longer life expectancy, but is also one of the best devices to lower family birth rates. It is obvious that when you have healthy children you do not need many children.

Since a woeful lack of health education in the home and the school has led to profound ignorance of even the elementary principles of personal hygiene and good nutrition, obviously the need for a minimum of health education in the schools—the basic do's and don'ts—cannot be overemphasized. A generation has already grown up since the country became free less than twenty-five years ago, and it is high time that we gave this matter our most urgent attention. Whatever amount is invested in education is bound to give disproportionately large dividends by preventing a plethora of minor and major ailments which plague our country. *As an underdeveloped country, what is India doing regarding curative aspects of building hospitals and medical colleges?*

Hospital equipment and care have suffered in quality. As for overcrowding in the district and even in some city hospitals, it has to be seen to be believed. Verandahs have been commandeered and numerous patients have to lie on the floor. Elementary conditions of hygiene and sanitation even in our hospitals are far from satisfactory. Some have isotopes but not fly swatters. A rapid increase in quantity in the face of limited resources in any sphere can only mean a serious impairment of quality.

And yet all the planning and expenditure on health development during the last two decades and more have been based on this misleading and obscurantist philosophy that the advancement of our people's health means more medical colleges and more hospital beds. This kind of effort ignores the causes of morbidity and mortality and concentrates on diagnosing, treating and attempting to cure the disease.

While a certain number of medical colleges and institutions for paramedical personnel as well as hospitals are certainly essential to treat the suffering and save the sick, it would be infinitely wiser and more economical to attack and eradicate as far as possible the root causes of our morbidity, still among the highest in the world.

Naturally we wish we had sufficient resources to have both adequate preventive and curative approaches. But unfortunately, underdeveloped countries constantly have to make difficult choices. And here the choice is between what is logical and what is not.

The proliferation of colleges and hospital beds has been impressive during the last twenty years but we have still been unable to give medical care to anywhere near all who need it, nor has the quality of care given been particularly high.

While in 1947, the year of India's political freedom, there were only 25 medical colleges with 1,983 admissions, there are today 94 medical colleges with a capacity to admit 12,000. This is a superior increase. During the Fourth Five-Year Plan period it is proposed to establish 10 more medical colleges and annual admissions are expected to go up to 13,000. But the existing colleges suffer from a lack of adequately trained teachers and equipment, and at least a score are frankly below par.

The number of doctors has increased from 47,524 in 1946-47 to 103,520 in 1969-70, with a resultant change in the doctor-population ratio from 1:6,300 to 1:5,112. At the end of the Fourth Five-Year Plan the number of doctors is expected to rise to 137,930 when the ratio will go up to 1:4,300, the desired norm being 1:3,500.

The number of nurses and auxiliary nurse midwives has witnessed similar proliferation during the last twenty years.

Should more attention and more resources be bestowed on the preventive and social aspects of medicine?

Yes. If half of the total amount expended by all the state governments was directed to the development of health infrastructures to cover total community health, nearly half of the existing morbidity might well disappear.

The kind of wasteful curative approach I am concerned about is pointed out by Dr. R. Mahadevan, chief medical officer in a tea plantation in South India. He writes:

When I took charge I found the medical officers indenting for chloromycetin in bulk day after day for treating cases of whooping cough among the estate children. Instead of pouring money on chloromycetin syrup we decided on the obvious alternative of "triple inoculations" of all children under two years. The incidence of whooping cough came down steeply, diphtheria has practically vanished and tetanus is a very rare occurrence.

An example of the type of preventive measure is the new "spray-gun injector," which is painless and does away entirely with needles and problems of sterilizing and can revolutionize immunization in our country, making it possible to immunize entire villages in a few hours. Here is where our money should go.

If my analysis of our morbidity and mortality pattern is accepted, then the only sensible, rational and effective way of meeting the health problem in India is to earnestly attack and eliminate the factors responsible for the incidence of these diseases.

What factors should the government emphasize?

The government and community must give top priority to:
1. provision of good drinking water
2. promotion of better environmental sanitation and public hygiene through effective disposal of wastes, provision of water-closet latrines in place of primitive dry latrines, and of underground sewage to replace open drainage

3. education of every child and adult in the basic principles of personal and public hygiene, nutrition and national fitness.

In a poor and developing country, far greater emphasis must be laid on preventive and social medicine than on diagnostic and curative services. And in the long run every rupee spent on the former will yield far greater dividends than the same rupee spent on curative services.

We have so much catching up to do with the advanced and affluent nations that we were tempted during the first five years of our development to try to copy, sometimes blindly, the medical situation in the developed countries. It was natural to think only of increasing medical and paramedical personnel and hospital beds during the last two decades in an effort to keep up with the inordinate growth of the population.

We in India are still at the first stage of controlling infectious and parasitic diseases. Roughly these account for a fourth of the total deaths. The more important causes in the group are tuberculosis of various forms, typhoid and tetanus. Malaria, which used to take a great toll of life, is now nearly under control, thanks to the work of the National Malaria Eradication Program.

Smallpox vaccination is obviously not yet universal, for smallpox continues to infect various parts of the country. Cholera, primarily a water-borne disease, is almost endemic in several parts of the country and often breaks out in epidemic form. Filariasis is still widely prevalent in the coastal regions. We have not so far successfully controlled the host of infective and parasitic diseases that characterize Indian morbidity and mortality and contribute much to lowering further the already weak resistance to disease.

India's infant mortality rate is more than 100 per 1,000 live births compared to 15-25 in the advanced countries.

While the causes of infant mortality in general range all the way from a garbage removers' strike to the foreign policy of a country which plunges it into war, they can be summarized in poverty, urbanization and poor health education. These are manifested in poor nutrition, undesirable environmental conditions and poor knowledge of mothercraft.

Customs and traditions and the entire cultural milieu which go counter to the principles of sound health have not been attacked successfully by a well-designed program of health education in schools, homes and if necessary even offices.

Among all the efforts to promote health—hospitals and dispensaries, control of communicable diseases, maternity and child health services and others—perhaps most effective and enduring is the health education of the people. All other services meet contingencies as they arise but health education lays a lasting foundation. If health education, given high priority, makes an effective impact, the people will themselves come forward for immunization, cultivate habits of personal and environmental sanitation and hygiene and look after their own nutritional needs.

Acute, chronic poverty is a barrier preventing millions of our people from reaching desirable nutritional standards. But it is possible, even within a very limited budget, to mitigate the rigors of unbalanced nutrition. For a large majority the problem is not poverty alone, but poverty coupled with ignorance.

Personal, religious and traditional inhibitions greatly hamper the development of a rational and scientific outlook and the adoption of a healthy way of life. Public health education should endeavor to remove these inhibitions. Any attempt to engineer behavioral changes is bound to be slow and arduous but it has to be undertaken, no matter what the obstacles. Resistance to reform that improves personal hygiene and public health must be changed, by the most subtle, intelligent and ingenious means we can devise, into readiness for innovation.

If India could have the amount now expended by the various state governments on the curative approach, and use this money to develop an effective and imaginative health structure, nearly half of our morbidity and mortality would soon disappear.

If the responsibility for all this is shared by the public, Christian missions and voluntary bodies, it will be possible to control the factors responsible for the poor health of our nation.

Is family planning a welfare measure?

Although family planning has its origins in the threat posed by rapidly growing numbers to our overall economic development and efforts to raise our level of living, it is no less a health and welfare measure.

A large family does not allow parents to give their children the necessary care for their physical, mental and emotional development. And if the small family becomes the norm, many health problems will be brought under control automatically. It may seem paradoxical but it is nevertheless true that in countries like Sweden a marked reduction in family size has led to a remarkably low infant mortality rate. If all the families in our country had no more than two or three children, many of our economic and social problems would vanish.

In tackling our population problem, prevention is certainly better than cure. Why bring children into this world who have no chances of survival beyond the age of one or five? And when they do survive, their chances of being assured all the decencies of civilized human life are far from certain. Every adult citizen who enters married life must swear allegiance to the concept of planned and responsible parenthood. Family planning is a health, economic and welfare measure including the total needs of people.

Christian missions in India began to provide welfare facilities mainly because of inadequacies of the former British administration in catering to total health needs. Christian missions abroad recognized and met the needs of the community and deservedly earned the gratitude of the people.

The significance of the services which mission hospitals have rendered is great because such service has no profit motive and, by and large, the beneficiaries are not charged anything. More than 20 percent of the total hospital bed strength in India belongs to Christian missionary hospitals.

It is a tribute to Christian missions that such services are rendered regardless of caste, creed or religion of those who seek medical relief. In our secular state, welfare activities can have meaning only when they are provided for the needy without any prejudice and discrimination.

---

india's new industrial fallacy

H. P. Nanda

What are some of India's new industrial goals?

India's new industrial policies are yet another demonstration of the frustration of Indian government-in-a-hurry. While it still uses the "socialistic" slogan as a peg to hang its political objectives on,

---

H. P. Nanda is a former member of Lok Sabha (lower house of the legislature), New Delhi.

With an exposure to the best of two worlds in medicine, it is my conviction that the expectations of Indian society are almost the same as in the United States despite various economic, cultural and social gaps.

—Paul M. Stephen, M.D.

the government is now awkwardly obvious about its lack of understanding of the industrial problem. One wonders if policymakers really mean business. The purpose of industrial policies in any economy—developing or developed—is to boost the gross national production. Policies and procedures are means to an end, and not an end by themselves. But our bureaucrats seem to derive a great pleasure in placing the cart before the horse as if to keep reassuring themselves that it is they who run the country and, as such, have prerogative to do as they do.

Our policies and regulations are only creating another class-unconsciousness among the industrial community, dividing it into isolated sectors, discriminating one against the other and perpetuating a constant state of confusion in our basic industrial objectives. All this, unfortunately, is done in the name of social reform. Misleading society is not "reforming." In fact, not leading society in the right direction is a deliberate act to mislead.

The real objectives of an industrial policy have to be based on socio-economic rather than just "social" considerations. Industrial production must increase progressively. And what makes industry flourish is free enterprise with a reward for its achievements, not mere policies or state controls, and certainly not any curbs on growth or size.

In the industrial system, growth is natural and goes to meet increasing costs of wages and raw materials. It is purely an economic proposition without which industry would collapse. It is impossible for any industry—big or small—to continue to give labor its annual increments and the minimum bonus, unless it earned this through increased output and growth.

The latest industrial policy displays the current government's size-complex in many forms. The theory that the new policy is "not industry-wise but investment-wise" is a lopsided approach to industrial development. The dividing line between various sectors in industry, according to this theory, is only the capital employed which, in fact, has no relationship with the break-even point that varies from industry to industry. This means that bureaucratic favor would remain on your side only as long as you made nuts and bolts but it would be withdrawn if you took up an industry such as automobiles, tractors or industrial machines. Who will then venture into those vital capital projects which are the fulcrum of industrial development anywhere in the world? Whose interest are these policies really serving? Obviously, it is neither the industry's nor the country's. Curb on diversification without license, as pronounced by the new industrial policy, is another unimaginative step and kills enterprise.

Has there been a prohibition against diversification?

On the one hand, the Finance Ministry encourages, through tax reliefs and incentives, the setting up of research and development departments in industries and on the other, the Ministry of Industrial Development is sitting with a whip in hand, ready to strike if you come up with a new product or innovation. What is the purpose of research and development, a costly exercise, if the fruits of this labor are forbidden?

Research and development, besides its social objectives of offering the customer the best and the latest for his utility, convenience or hygiene, provides the industry with an alternative to switch over to new products during recessionary periods, as being faced by diesel engine and pump industries at present, or when a product has lived its life cycle. Instead of depriving the industry of this lifeboat, the government should make sure that all new industrial projects must close down if they cannot diversify in time. Apart from what it means to the stockholders, of which even government institutions are a part, it is a national loss to let plants close down in this manner.

Does the government permit entrepreneurs licenses for articles developed by them on their own initiative and through their own research efforts?

India's licensing system seems to be in a hurry to freeze the industrial process at a stage where some Indian companies are just beginning to turn towards mass production. In fact, we have hardly anything near mass production, compared to world production standards. Yet it is creditable that some Indian products have penetrated foreign markets. Restrictions on capacities of the so-called "large" units—the pioneering industries which braved two difficult decades to reach where they are today—is a step neither democratic nor productivity oriented.

Often we are asked to follow Japan's example in the development of small scale industries. Well, it is established all over the world, including Japan, that small scale industries can best flourish as ancillaries to large industries. They should be given a complementary role rather than reservations or concessions which kill competition and, therefore, quality-consciousness. Even in Japan, where small scale industries constitute 99.4 percent of all manufacturing units, the industrial output of large scale units is almost 50 percent of the total production. It is obvious that unless the large capital units grow, the small industries could never flourish.

Delays have become proverbial with our licensing system. The Foreign Investment Board was set up to expedite the foreign collaboration agreements within the guidelines of investment ratios and royalties. But it is a pity that, although the concerned ministries and departments are represented in the FIB, decisions go back and forth for years on minor, sometimes meaningless, queries, thus throwing the production programs completely out of gear. Implementation of the rules and regulations is more in letter than in spirit and the process is generally slow. These delays sometimes get so frustrating that the foreign collaborators want to withdraw in midstream. Even if an honest, objective government officer takes some initiative in settling a straightforward case promptly, he is suspected of favor and being involved with the entrepreneur.

Are there controls by the government?

There is an endless chain of checks and controls around private industry. Referring particularly to products under the price control purview, the government formula for price fixation allows a maximum return of 12 percent on fixed assets plus working capital. The more fixed assets one had—whether or not utilized—the better the return allowed. In other words, the government costing formula gives a premium on inefficiency. An industry which tries to help the ancillary units by purchasing components from them and assembling these components into a finished product would always stand at a disadvantage under this cost formula, compared to another unit which manufactures all these components itself, as the latter would get a higher return in view of higher volume of fixed assets involved.

Even more anomalous, there is no price control for the ancillary industry. Prices of ancillary components keep rising more frequently than the pace of price revision in the capital goods industry. The latter can be tragically caught between the upward thrust of ancillary prices from below and the fixed ceiling on the sale prices of the end products from above. Such a costing formula is a sudden departure in practice from what government tries to preach in helping small scale industry. Large industries are forced by this formula to make as many components as they can themselves. The costing formula is helping neither small scale industry nor capital goods industry.

Does current taxation include a high rate of property tax?

There is an additional urban property tax and a ceiling on total income. Beyond a certain degree of growth, there is no incentive for industry to perform better. There are hardly any incentives left, except for a sense of national obligation, for the so-called big industrialists and the capable directors and managers in the corporate sector to work more. The much publicized fear that private sector can exploit is a myth. For, in the present corporate power system, no individual or group of individuals can take away any profits without paying a good share of taxes.

Is there a concentration of economic power?

Concentration of economic power has been overplayed to the extent of making successful private ventures look like social pests rather than national assets. Large industrial groups are pioneers of India's industry. These groups have fought for the country a more difficult battle for economic freedom than the politicians' struggle for political freedom. The only difference is that they never sought election to Parliament, nor indulged in slogan-mongering. If government cannot use these pioneering leaders of industry for their contribution to the country's economy—in terms of employment of millions, valuable research for new products and services and enormous tax contribution towards the national exchequer—let them, at least, not be called black sheep.

What is really ailing us? Is our bureaucracy success-shy? Or is it lack of perspective in the policy-maker's eye? Both are dangerous symptoms for our country's economic progress.

NEW HORIZONS FOR INDIA'S WOMEN

take lachmi, for instance

Chanda Christdas

Is the role of women less binding in India today?

In the cities and among the educated elite, traditional limitations on social contact and the role of women are less binding now than they once were. But four out of five Indians still live in rural villages where the impact of any social or economic change is slow, and the vast majority of people born into this most durable of ancient civilizations are still bound by the role society dictates for them.

Take Lachmi, for instance, a girl I would judge to be no more than thirteen. Often she passed me in the street, her sari dusty and tied carelessly back, a flat basket of bricks, gravel or concrete balanced on her head. She works regularly at a construction site, earning about thirty-two cents a day. Though her appearance is that of a street urchin, she wears the gold ornaments of a married woman.

One evening I met her without her accustomed burden. She was scrubbed and dressed in fresh clothes, and from her animated expression I guessed she was on her way to a celebration. I asked her what the occasion was.

"I am going to my mother's house tonight. The family of the man who wishes to marry my sister will be coming with gifts for her. They will bring flowers and fruit. When we accept the gifts, it will mean that she is promised in marriage."

Miss Christdas works for the United Methodist Board of Missions, Methodist House, Hyderabad.

*If you study history,
you will find that
where women have
risen, that country
attained a high
position, and
wherever they
remained dormant,
that country
slipped back.*
—*Indira Gandhi*

"How old is she?" I asked.

"She is ten years old."

"How old were you, Lachmi, when you married?"

"I was much younger than she."

"Lachmi, do you know that the government has established by law that girls are not to be married younger than sixteen or boys before they are eighteen?"

Lachmi laughed at this. "I know of families where girls are given in marriage at four or five."

"Is it wise," I asked her, "to marry a young child to an older man with whom she must spend the rest of her life?"

Lachmi considered for only a moment. "It is a good custom. She will go back and forth between her home and her husband's home. He and she will grow and play together as brother and sister. My husband and I did the same. We are loving and happy together. The unfortunate ones are these modern girls. They flirt with several boys. Some are ruined before they are married. Often they are unhappy. Their marriages don't last."

Does child marriage continue to exist among the well-to-do families?

The custom of child marriage is found not only in circumstances like Lachmi's where ignorance and poverty lock succeeding generations into this tradition, but often in well-to-do, liberal families where the custom is observed in spite of legal prohibition. Muslims claim that the Koran prescribes that a father should arrange marriage for his daughter when she reaches the age of twelve or be blamed thereafter if she falls into sin.

The practice of early marriage among Hindus became common during the medieval period of successive invasions. Girls were considered safer from violation or capture if they were married. At the beginning of British rule, eight or nine years was the common marriage age; and early betrothal is still practiced in India, especially among Brahmins, where it is strictly observed. Sometimes there is an enormous difference in age of husband and wife.

Marriage by parental arrangement is practiced all over India. Many young people who are otherwise modern are content with the ease and security of this custom. However, increased education, foreign degrees and freedom of movement have given others the confidence to choose their own mates.

When a marriage is to be arranged, parents consult marriage makers who are familiar with the family background and position. Social, financial and educational factors are considered in making a match. An astrologer may be called in to compare horoscopes for compatibility of temperaments and to study the omens in making wedding plans.

Dr. Srinivas Rao, in spite of studying and living in New York and practicing medicine in a Jewish hospital, went back to India to be married to one of the three graduates whom his parents had selected. To a certain extent it was an arranged marriage. After his return to the United States he was asked on what basis he had selected his bride. He replied, "She was gentle and shy in her manners and seemed to be humble and obedient." The average Indian boy wants his wife to be obedient and gentle. Dr. Rao was merely following custom in choosing such a girl for his wife.

The Hindu marriage ceremony itself is solemn but brief, a symbolic circling of a fire (hearth) by the couple in the presence of a priest and assembled family and caste members. To present the newlywed couple to the village in which they live, a procession is organized, including fireworks, musicians, dancers and lamp bearers. This public entertainment and an accompanying reception and banquet in the bride's house makes the celebration very expensive. Often the family goes deeply in debt to finance it, but the display is considered to be essential as a matter of family prestige.

Among poorer people there is not so much ceremony, but even for them the wedding day is special. It may be the only day in their lives when they do not feel the pinch of poverty. Great sacrifices are made to present the grandest, most elaborate feast possible.

The custom of giving a dowry with a daughter is also common, especially in South India. Often parents borrow money for their daughter's bride present and spend the next ten or twenty years repaying it.

Is the joint family tradition a patriarchal system?

Child marriage is one of a related group of traditions that also includes the institution of an extended family in one patriarchal household. Such a household may include three generations living under the same roof: parents, grown sons, their wives and children and unmarried daughters. This style of living is not confined to backward or rural areas. The following census report is quoted from the *Deccan Chronicle* of April 14, 1971:

There are 86 members in one single family, residing under one roof in Hyderabad, the recent census operations revealed. . . . The Director of Census Operations said that the head of the family was a high-placed government official.

To searching questions put by the perplexed enumerator as to whether different families with different establishments were staying in the house, the official stiffly replied that he was the head of the one single family of 86 and was responsible for their maintenance.

The late Nizam of Hyderabad had two sons by his legal wife and more than a hundred by his 60 to 100 concubines. As though this were not sufficient, he adopted more than a hundred poor children, the entire family living in the palace. Since the Nizam was a wealthy prince, he was able to supply food, clothes and schooling for his own and his adopted children. When they grew up, he arranged their marriages one by one, provided their livelihoods, built separate cottages near the palace and created trust funds for their support. Most Muslims who were in the Nizam's service have followed his example in having large joint households.

The joint family gives its members social and economic security. It preserves racial, caste and social groupings and enables the young to marry early. Its best feature is the cultivation and maintenance of sympathy and good feelings among its members. In a joint family there is a closeness and solidarity which can be utilized for worship and stewardship of talents. The joint family can exist because of the pooling of work and income by all the males, often all working at the same trade or business, or farming.

An excellent illustration of economic security in a joint family is the story of the Kapoors, recently written up in *The Illustrated Weekly of India* under the title "The Fabulous Kapoors." This family of actors came into prominence early in the century with Prithviraj Kapoor, for whom the Prithvi theater in India is named. His sons Raj, Shammi and Sashi are all successful film actors. Two grandsons, Randhir and Rishi, have already appeared in films as youngsters. The Prithvi theater not only stimulated a renaissance in Hindustani theater, but gave impetus to a distinct Indian style of movie making.

In an Indian village it is common practice for the father to pass on his inherited trade to his sons and grandsons. Carpenters, blacksmiths, masons, tailors and weavers often inherit not only their skills but the customers their fathers served.

This joint family system is more common in rural areas, and the courtyard of a village house is the center of activity. Here the women of the household spend all their time cleaning and grinding grain into flour, pounding chilies into powder, mending clothes, taking care of babies, cooking and feeding the cattle that live in a corner of the courtyard.

These women are held in subordinate, dependent positions. They act as domestic servants to their husbands and children, but their task is considered noble and their position by no means despised. A mother is deeply respected and loved. She has considerable authority in the home. In wealthier families the wife's responsibility is limited to supervision of the household, but in poorer homes she carries on all household duties and often works outside the home as well, tending crops, carrying sand, earth and bricks at construction sites, hiring out as a houseworker or, more rarely, as an office worker.

While there may be great advantages in a joint family system, there are equally many disadvantages. Quarrels may arise between brothers and between generations. Autocratic mothers-in-law may treat daughters-in-law cruelly. Because of the authoritarian position of the father or the elder brother, there is no scope for the development of responsibility or individuality. There is much less parental influence on a child since discipline and direction come from a large number of adults. Relationships can become confused or hostile in such a situation.

Polygamy is not as common as it once was, but even now a man whose wife produces no son may bring a second, third or fourth wife into the home, hoping for male issue. Polyandry is not en-

tirely unknown in India. The *Mahābhārata* tells the legend of Drāupadi, whose fate was to marry the five Pāndava brothers. This custom is still practiced among certain hill tribes and low castes of the Deccan plateau. In Kerala, among Nayyars, children take the name of their mother; inheritance is through her line rather than that of her husband. A husband in this group has no rights over his wife's family and may even be displaced in favor of another man.

Although officially the caste system has been abolished in India, in practice it is still generally observed, particularly in the distinguishing practices of various subgroups who continue in vegetarian or other dietary habits, standards and rituals of cleanliness, proscriptions against tobacco and alcohol, or traditions regarding inheritance of property, sequestering of women and degrees of religious orthodoxy. However, to a certain extent caste barriers are easing. Inter-caste marriage is no longer uncommon. Some Christians have married into Hindu or Muslim families. A few socially or politically prominent families have allowed inter-caste or inter-religious marriages of their children.

Is divorce permitted?

Apart from a few sects which permit divorce and remarriage, marriage in India is considered a permanent union. The only legal ground for divorce is adultery. In Hinduism high value is placed on a virtuous woman. Divorce and remarriage are socially unacceptable. Traditionally a widow was not allowed to remarry. A girl married in early childhood might lose her husband without ever having known him, but she was nevertheless considered a widow, condemned to remain at home all her life, dressed in white without any ornaments or jewelry, forbidden to take any direct part in public festivities.

This strict attitude has been fiercely contested and successfully overcome in some cases. But the high value placed on female virtue has made many widows unwilling to consider remarriage. Earlier, a woman's faithfulness was exemplified by the now outlawed practice of *sati,* or ritual suicide, in which the widow cast herself on the funeral pyre of her husband.

Among Muslims divorce is more acceptable. A divorce can be obtained after a separation of four months, and it is expected that the husband will make a generous settlement on his former wife. Both partners may marry again, or the husband may take his divorced wife back. There has been some government pressure toward giving women equal rights in marriage, inheritance and employment.

Have changes moved toward liberalizing restrictive traditions?

In general, the movement in India is toward liberalization of restrictive traditions of caste, marriage and family hierarchy. Changes have been introduced by the coming of independence, by economic necessity, by legislative measures, by the availability of schooling and by freer social contact. Some traditions, such as the authoritarian family unit of three generations, are losing influence. City living makes this impractical. The poverty and unemployment of the countryside limit the practice to prosperous high caste landowners, and sons now leave home to seek employment in industrial areas or foreign countries.

The impact of family planning on the traditional family structure will be felt in coming years. India has given high priority to population control in recent planning. Under the current Five-Year Plan expenditures for birth control programs are expected to increase sharply. There are now 34,000 rural family planning centers as well as 800 mobile units for sterilization and for fitting of intrauterine devices. The effort is intended to keep India's population increase within manageable proportions so that expected gains in food production will begin to have an impact on the general health and economy of the country.

Rapid social change is sweeping across India. Men and women are reexamining their roles in an industrial society to come. The tendency is to disregard previously accepted values and social structures in an effort to cope with radically altered personal and social circumstances. The coming generation is entering adulthood with much more education. Their attitudes are more fluid; they see their roles evolving, as men and women and as people in society.

---

poor women's liberation

Mary Alexander

Has the women's liberation movement reached India?

To a certain extent. It is just starting because Indian independence came so late—even though women also took an active role in the freedom movement. When we did achieve our independence, equal rights were given to both male and female. So there is not so much to fight for. Women want to be recognized as equal partners, not as common chattel. Among the educated classes, I think men are willing to listen to women in every field. Maybe the man is stronger than the woman physically, but mentally in any field the woman is even more alert. We find at the YWCA—es-

---

Miss Alexander is Youth Secretary, Young Women's Christian Association, Madras.

> *As a general rule the horizon of the Indian woman is bound by the four walls of her courtyard. She is taught the truth that the highest ideal of life is service, but to her so often that means service only to her husband and her family.*
>
> —*G. S. Dutt*

pecially in Madras, a very conservative city—that women are much more progressive, much more forward. They are ten steps ahead of men with new ideas, innovations, new ways of thinking. Women are open to new ideas. The YW does work that men's organizations do. Men tend to be overly cautious; they don't like change. But women are in the forefront here. So although there is need for more liberation, women here don't have to fight for it as such because men realize that they need them to go forward.

Are there any signs of the women's liberation movement penetrating villages where liberation is most needed?

Well, in the villages, you find that women work a lot. It is very hard for a family to live, and unless women work hard they cannot afford to survive. So the man takes the woman as his partner in his work, always in the fields to help him with, for example, the harvesting. He does half the work and she does the other half.

You come in contact with many types of students at the YWCA. What are your impressions of hippies?

I think it is easy to generalize, to call anybody a *hippie* just because he grows long hair. One aspect that I like about hippies is that they are searching; they realize that there is something lacking in their lives and they go from place to place searching for something to make their lives more meaningful. They seem to be willing to go to any place and if need be even suffer or undergo any amount of discomfort just to discover what it is that is needed in their lives.

Is this sense of searching reflected in most youth today?

Yes. I find that they are always questioning, especially our modern Indian youth. For example, at Madras University, students refuse to accept anything which is handed down to them. They question and then evaluate it. In the process some may get terribly mixed up because they don't have answers to questions they pose—but nobody else does either. Many of our elders pose the same questions. They don't have clear answers either. Many questions are posed—but no answers are being offered.

What can the YWCA really do to help the youth of India?

Well, the YWCA is definitely a women's liberation organization. It must continue to encourage women to be independent human beings. For example, women in India have strongly opposed the idea of uniting the YWCA and YMCA.

Women have opposed uniting with the men because they feel women are quite capable of running organizations. Where the YWCA and YMCA have merged in other nations, in most offices the man is director and the woman is just an ordinary secretary. Often her talent is absolutely wasted. But when you have two separate organizations, women maintain equality. Therefore, women are dead set against joining with the men and that, I think, is a real liberation movement. Many people who are YWCA members end up being leaders in social work. So you see, our Indian women are unafraid to think for themselves and risk going ahead and doing the uncommon.

---

family planning— three or two or one or none

S. N. Agarwala

What does the red triangle poster symbolize?

The red triangle on our posters symbolizes family planning. Since it was first adopted five years ago, millions of red triangles

---

Dr. Agarwala is Director of the International Institute for Population Studies, Bombay.

Based on an article in *The Illustrated Weekly of India,* Feb. 7, 1971. Used by permission.

have been distributed all over India. They have been painted on buses, walls, buildings, trees, trains, etc. In one state an elephant was used for carrying huge red triangles. One enterprising young man glued red triangles on his kites! Songs, dramas and folk dances have also been utilized. The slogan which earlier was "Two or three children" has now changed to "We two, our two."

What has this slogan accomplished?

It certainly has created an atmosphere in favor of family planning and has increased general awareness. It is said that about 80 percent of the people in the urban areas and between 60 and 70 percent in the rural areas are aware of family planning. But awareness is not sufficient. What is required is that the small family should become a way of life for the people of India. In India a couple produces six or seven children. In other words, two gets multiplied and becomes eight or nine. In the modern, developed countries, two often remains two. This is mainly due to the widespread practice of contraception in developed countries, and not to any difference in the capacity to bear children. In India only about 7 percent of the reproductive couples in the age group of 18-45 use contraceptives; in the Western countries the number of contraceptive users is between 90 and 100 percent.

Eighty-three percent of India's population lives in villages. The rural people are still tradition bound and their level of literacy is very low. Many still think that a large number of children is a sign of virility, that male children are a source of strength in the event of a quarrel, that more children mean more hands in the fields, especially when hired labor gets scarce at times of harvesting and higher wages are demanded. The cost of a child has not entered their calculations—a child requires very few clothes and food costs little as it is grown in the fields. A smaller population may be advantageous to the country and may hasten the process of development, but an average villager cannot visualize how a smaller family will be economically advantageous to him. This is the crux of the problem, which is holding up the rapid spread of family planning in rural India. It must be explained to a villager that family planning is economically advantageous to him. This can be done through personal contacts and small group meetings by leaders and family planning workers. There are four distinct stages of the motivational process—awareness, knowledge, trial and practice.

What are mass media doing to motivate family planning awareness?

It is known that the mass media help in taking people to awareness stage only, and their role in later stages is insignificant. Through personal contact and small group meetings people are brought from awareness to practice. A great deal of effort, therefore, has to be concentrated in this area. The role of pamphlets, posters, wall paintings, etc., in a country where illiteracy is very high is bound to be low. Also, different groups of people living in an area, and people living in different parts of India, have different attitudes, and therefore the content of the motivational campaign has to differ from one group to another. The message has to be carried out by local leaders and conveyed through the medium of local dialect, in words readily understood by the people.

Although the current use of modern contraceptives in the villages is very small, one should not get the impression that village people are opposed to limiting the size of their families, or that it would be very difficult to convert them in its favor. A majority of the villagers know about coitus interruptus and continence. Village women know about the rhythm method, although the safe days are often not calculated accurately. They also have faith in a number of rituals, the observance of which they think protects them from early conception. For instance, in some villages around Delhi, the woman counts the beams of the ceiling of the room at the time of delivery, and if she is able to count three, she believes that her next child will be born three years later, and if two, after two

This birth control poster is a familiar sight in India.

years. Again, some believe that if only the floor of the room where the child is born is plastered after childbirth, the next child will be born after one year, but if the walls are also plastered, the interval will be between two and three years.

It is easy to laugh at the simplicity and naiveté of these women. But the important fact that emerges is that they are not completely unaware that it is possible to space out children, and they make efforts to increase the interval between births. Surveys have also shown that village women resort to prolonged breast feeding with the same objective. Some are known to use herbs which are said to be abortifacients. All this suggests that village women should be given correct knowledge about family planning methods and how to use them. Needless to say, the contraceptives must be simple, inexpensive and easily available. Village women will not take readily to modern contraceptives, and likely will be more willing to use indigenous drugs or herbs as contraceptives. Research in this area is urgently needed.

What medium of communication should be utilized to effect family planning?

Studies indicate that a very powerful medium is the village gossip. Women, when they go to fetch water from the village well or to take a bath, or go out in groups to defecate, and men while they sit in the *chaupal*, like to chat about new and novel things. If the family planning action-workers successfully pick up topics which are unusual and interesting, they can tickle the curiosity of the village people and generate a "multiplier effect"—those who hear will carry the message to others. Such programs might considerably increase the popularity of family planning in rural areas.

It is also necessary to provide services at the door. It is too much to ask a villager to walk five to ten miles to a family planning clinic to get a contraceptive. Mobile vans, which will visit villages at regular intervals, are required. Family planning is not a medical problem; it is an integral part of the process of social and economic development. Therefore, it should not be expected that if family planning clinics are opened, people will visit them for contraceptive services as they would go to a hospital if they were ill. Doctors engaged in family planning work have to adopt an attitude of service, and take the role of social reformers in convincing people to use contraceptives.

In recent years, the eyes of the world have been focused on

India's population problems. India's population is about 550 million; nearly 1.7 million people are added each month. At the present rate of growth, India's population might nearly double itself and become one billion by the year 2000. If, however, family planning becomes successful, the billion mark may be reached ten to fifteen years later. The consequences of doubling the present population in the next twenty to thirty years can well be imagined. Since independence, food production has increased by about 70 percent and industrial production by 150 percent, but the average Indian does not feel the benefit of this development very much. An estimated 15-20 million people are unemployed in India and nearly 65 million children of school age are not in school. Per capita food production has tended to decrease and there is a shortage of nearly one million houses. Population limitation in India, therefore, is an important variant between poverty and prosperity, hunger and nonhunger, political stability and instability and fulfillment and nonfulfillment of the expectations of future generations.

Is family planning really possible?

The present rate of growth is the highest recorded so far. Since 1921 India's population has more than doubled, and since independence it has increased by about 200 million. The increase has been largely due to a decline in the death rate, and not to an increase in the birth rate. Our death rate has become quite low, and in the next ten years or so, it will reach the level of 10 per 1,000 population, the current level in some developed countries. The future growth of India's population will depend upon the trends in birth rate. If a sufficient number of reproductive couples start using contraceptives, the birth rate might fall and the rate of population growth decline. Prevailing factors—a very young population, low age at marriage, lower incidence of widowhood due to declining mortality, higher widow remarriages, declining length of lactation period and growing immigration of Indians settled abroad—all favor a higher birth rate. The task of population limitation has not only become more vital for the future prosperity of the people of India, but also increasingly difficult.

What is the minimum goal India should try to meet every year?

Out of 550 million Indians, nearly 100 million are couples in the age group 15-45, generally the age of reproduction. This number is not static; in fact it continues to increase. Each year nearly 5.5

> *I do not regard myself as a woman. I am
> a person with a job.*
>
> —*Indira Gandhi*

million new couples enter reproductive age while some 2.5 million die or cross the age of 45 and become unreproductive. The number of reproductive couples increases annually by about 3 million. If we desire to reduce our birth rate in a period of ten years the number of contraceptive users should be around 4 million in the first year and increase to about 93 million in the tenth year. In other words, around 90 percent of reproductive couples must eventually become effective users of contraceptives.

If all couples restrict their children to three, nearly 9 million births will not take place each year. This is the rationale behind the government of India's slogan of having not more than three children. But this reduction in the birth rate would be possible only when no couple has more than three children and contraceptives are used by all couples.

What has India achieved so far?

Although social reformers and family planning enthusiasts in India were pleading for a population control policy as early as the twenties, the government adopted the policy of population control only in 1951. But little was accomplished until 1964-65. The total number of sterilization operations carried out before 1951 was only one million. The program has shown considerable progress since, especially during the period 1965-70 when 5.7 million sterilizations were performed and 3.1 million IUDs inserted. Since some of these must have crossed the reproductive age or died, the number of couples currently protected through sterilization and IUDs is estimated to be around 6 million. In addition, 70-80 million pieces of Nirodh (condom) and 3 million pieces of other conventional contraceptives were distributed during 1969-70.

In the absence of adequate information, it is not possible to calculate the actual users of conventional contraceptives, since it is not known how much of the quantity distributed is actually used and with what degree of regularity. The government estimates that current users of Nirodh are around 3.5 million. This, however, appears to be a generous estimate.

Couples currently protected in India appear to be around 8 million, or 8 percent of the reproductive couples. This is a far cry from the target of more than 90 percent. It is worth remembering that of those sterilized, a majority have more than three children and, therefore, the impact on birth reduction is not as significant as it would have been if they had not had children before sterilization.

The impression that we are not doing as well in family planning as we wish is undisputed. In fact one gets depressed when it is realized that there has been a steady decline in the achievement of targets since 1967-68, the only year in which the targets were fully achieved. It is unfortunate that 1967-68, which should have been a threshold for a steady upward jump, has tended to become a year of peak achievement.

Voluntary service and the cafeteria approach are the unique features of our family planning program. Certain steps which might hasten progress cannot be adopted as they are against the democratic conscience of our country. This makes the task all the more difficult and challenging. The conditions under which the present-day developed countries could bring about a demographic transition from high to low fertility do not prevail in India, and therefore their experience is not of much practical value in the execution of our program. The near continental size of the population of India and the great variety of people and problems forbid any unique solution of the problem. Legislation raising the minimum age of female marriages, introduction of population education in primary schools and sex education in higher secondary schools, liberalizing of abortion and so forth might have some effect provided people are motivated and willing to undertake measures to reduce the size of their families.

For India there is no escape from population limitation and there is no easy way to achieve it. The climate, both national and international, is in favor of family planning and there is no shortage of funds. We can certainly make more rapid progress.

LAND–
A GIFT OF GOD

**fertilizers, water, tractors, pride:
the green revolution**

M. S. Randhawa

How did the Green Revolution, which you helped initiate, start?

The Green Revolution, which has been going on for a decade now in Punjab, was due basically to enlightened leadership. Most of the government officials are themselves farmers so they appreciate the needs and problems of farmers That's why they gave this agricultural scheme very high priority. The droughts in 1964 and 1966 were devastating but they proved a blessing in disguise —people learned that unless they had a secure source of irrigation in the form of tube wells, they could get nothing from their fields. So this led to sinking of more tube wells. Now there are 160,000 tube wells in Punjab, half of which are electrified and half powered by diesel engines.

Another milestone in the Green Revolution was in the use of fertilizers. In this part of Punjab, there was very little use of fertilizers. People depended mostly on farmyard manure for fertilizing their fields. But this can never be sufficient for a large area, so only one-third of the land was really fertilized and the rest had to go without any type of fertilizer. And this deficiency could only be made up by chemical fertilizers, which were popularized from 1965 onwards.

But then an important development took place. We selected irrigated districts all over India, and made arrangements for a supply of chemical fertilizers to all these areas. Remarkable things happened. Last year the production of wheat was over 20 million

Dr. Randhawa is Vice Chancellor of the Punjab Agricultural University, Ludhiana.

tons. Such a large increase in grain production had never taken place before in history; that's why it can be given no other name but *Green Revolution.*

The Green Revolution was also promoted by a scheme under which the government gave incentive prices to farmers. This is most important because cultivation of wheat means heavy expenditure. A farmer must apply heavy dosages of fertilizers, he must irrigate these wheat fields about seven times during their period of growth, then he has to hoe them by hand. All of this means a heavy outlay. Now as soon as the crop is ready, farmers harvest it, then straightway market it. So the problem of storing it on farm land has gone.

Many changes in farming have also taken place. Formerly most of the wheat was threshed by people beating it under the feet of their bullocks. Now most is threshed mechanically by threshers, which are run on electric motors or by tractors or diesel engines. The number of tractors is also increasing. About 200,000 tractors are required in Punjab alone, and about 50,000 are in use.

Are tractors manufactured in India?

Yes, but not in any great number. In two or three years this manufacturing problem will be much easier. But in the meantime, under the World Bank loan, about 8,000 tractors will be imported, which should be very useful to the Punjab farmers.

But can the farmer afford fuel for tractors?

Farmers who can purchase tractors usually can afford fuel. And the fuel which is most preferred is diesel oil.

Is there anything that a country like America can do to help in the continuation of this Green Revolution?

America has already given India much help. Whenever there was a shortage of wheat in India, the Mexican varieties of wheat developed by Dr. Norman Ernest Borlaug of the Rockefeller Foundation were given by the U.S.A. and were of immense assistance.

In 1966, the Punjab Agricultural University established a cooperative arrangement with Ohio State University, which has been a great help. We send staff and graduates to Ohio for Ph.D. work in subjects in which we lack facilities. American scientists also work with us at Ludhiana where Indians teach Americans.

At Punjab Agricultural University farmers continue to come for

advice. We have an extension department devoted entirely to this work. About 20,000 selected farmers who want to learn are brought to the university where they are taught techniques regarding various crops, from the selection of seed to harvesting. We have a farmers' hostel which has accommodations for 200 men, and short courses are given in tractor driving, the use of machinery, poultry farming and crop raising. Farmers and ex-military men who are going into farming come to learn from these courses.

In summary, the Green Revolution will require more mechanical devices. America has 5 million tractors. That explains why American agriculture is so efficient. With only a couple of men, farmers with adequate machinery can manage large areas of land. Certainly our farmers require more tractors and farm machinery, so that their work is done with ease and efficiency.

grow more food:
the green revolution

V. P. Naik

What were some of the handicaps India faced in starting the Green Revolution?

In 1947 India was handicapped by the fact that on Partition, a large chunk of fertile and irrigated land went to Pakistan. The vagaries of the monsoon made our position still more difficult. The Grow More Food Campaign had only partial success. The British had appointed a number of royal commissions on agriculture who made suggestions which remained on paper. Before the British quit India, in 1943, we had the harrowing experience of the Bengal famine in which 3.5 million people perished. It was only after we became free that we earnestly took up the quest for self-sufficiency in food.

Since it was the responsibility of the government of a free India to ensure food to its people, it imported food grains on a large scale. This inhibited plans for economic progress. Then, in 1966-67, came the Bihar famine, which stung our conscience and awakened us again to our pathetic dependence on outside aid.

Why couldn't India, an agricultural country, produce enough food?

Not only was the increase in production year by year little (in some years there was a fall in production), it was hopelessly unable to catch up with the growth of population. We were producing more babies than cereals. Even a gigantic family planning program could not stem the surging rise in population.

Other countries, advanced in industry and not predominantly agricultural, were producing more food than India, and a much higher yield per acre. Why not India? The question was a challenge to the government. New strains of cereals were being developed and tried in foreign research centers. These had brought about a green revolution in a number of countries, one revolution we were eager to import. And we decided to do it.

Who was the leader of the Green Revolution?

The leader was Dr. Norman Ernest Borlaug; and his weapon

The Honorable V. P. Naik is Chief Minister, Maharashtra.

was Mexican wheat. India imported Mexican seeds and thereby sowed the seeds of the Green Revolution in the country. Our agricultural institutions and their scientists played a part in propagating this revolution. The results were spectacular.

The estimated food grain production for all India in 1947-48 was 52.8 million tons; in 1969-70 it was 99.5 million tons. In twenty-three years we have managed nearly to double the output. This has been accomplished in a variety of ways, but primarily by the use of better seeds and increased inputs of water and fertilizers.

The size of our land holdings may seem a handicap in introducing mechanized farming. But in countries like Japan and Taiwan production is very high despite the small farms. Many states have made provisions for the consolidation of holdings. Cooperative farming has also helped in mechanization. Tractors are being used increasingly. Harvesters and power tillers are also in use.

As a result of the new strategy adopted in 1966-67, India has achieved near self-sufficiency in food over a period of three years. This strategy consists of cultivation of high-yielding varieties, use of adequate fertilizers and pesticides, multiple cropping, irrigation and intensive cultivation, soil and water management, research and its application, farmers' training, development of credit, marketing and distribution arrangement for the supply of inputs, adoption of price policies for better production.

It is evident that this strategy has yielded good results. There is every reason to hope that India will become self-sufficient by 1972.

Is there a breakthrough in rice?

Critics of the Green Revolution say that it is confined to wheat. The food problem in India is basically a problem of rice. The trouble with this cereal is that in any emergency, unlike wheat, the availability of imports is limited. Before World War II, we used to import from Burma one or two million tons of rice. The rice position became critical during the war and in the following years. Our efforts since independence have been rewarding. Between 1948 and 1970 we have nearly doubled production—from 21.58 million tons to 40.43 million tons.

According to the chairman of the National Commission on Agriculture, a green revolution in rice is possible within the next two or three years. In 1970 progress was made in evolving new high-yielding dwarf varieties.

So far we have been talking of quantity. More attention should be paid to the quality of the food we eat. A nation's physical strength and intellectual capacity depend on the protein intake of its citizens. Growing children must be assured of adequate protein. For this purpose our production of milk, eggs, fish and poultry must increase at a faster rate. Horticulture can be pursued by all citizens. It need not be confined to the professional farmer.

What is the real leveler of land?

Water, I feel, is the real leveler of land. Famine could be abolished from India forever if 40 percent of the land was irrigated. Maharashtra, for example, can double its production if all its water resources are effectively tapped. At present only about 8 percent of the cropped area is irrigated, although 11 percent of the area under food grains in India is in Maharashtra. The Punjab is in a favorable position because it has the best irrigation facilities. Provided with adequate funds for more irrigation projects our state, too, will show good results in agriculture. As it is, supplies from outside are already on the decrease. In a normal year (the monsoon being favorable), Maharashtra produces enough to feed itself.

Land reforms and the fixation of ceilings (in Maharashtra the ceilings vary from 18 acres to 126 acres, according to the type of land) have been beneficial. The elimination of intermediaries has been a blessing, along with fixity of tenure. Our price policy is based on a rational principle. To increase production, the farmer must be given an incentive, i.e., remunerative prices, and these must be assured throughout the year. Our monopoly procurement scheme serves two purposes: fair prices to the grower and unfailing supply to the consumer. In addition, unscrupulous middlemen are prevented from taking advantage of scarcity.

What does the Maharashtra government do in times of scarcity?

Dues and land revenue are suspended. Short-term loans given to peasants are converted to medium-term loans. Our experience is that the borrower does not default, because the credit enables him to be a more efficient farmer. Financial relief ensures at least the second year's crop. If there is acute drought and stoppage of cultivation, we provide work at centers in the neighborhood— digging small tanks, soil conservation, roads and construction of tube wells.

The common Indian farmer is born poor, lives poor and dies poor. Only the affluent farmers can afford capital investment and produce a surplus for the market. . . . Some of the best land is owned by people who have other gainful employment, but hold it as a security for old age. Therefore, the tenant, or sharecropper, is not able to take advantage of the Green Revolution.

—Dr. M. J. John

In Maharashtra, land in which cereals and millets are grown has not been diverted to cash crops. However, I am of the view that cash crops cannot be neglected in view of their importance to the economy. The sensible thing is to grow in an area what can grow best there. Maharashtra's acreage of some cash crops in relation to all India is as follows: cotton, 36.11 percent; groundnut, 13.82 percent; sugarcane, 8.25 percent.

You remember how the 1965 drought produced a depression in our economy, crippling our engineering industry. (We have not yet fully recovered.) The lesson it retaught us is that agriculture is the base of our industry. Without raw materials no industries can thrive. The present Green Revolution has already had its impact on various industrial sectors. The purchasing capacity of the farmer has gone up, creating increased demands for consumer goods. The Green Revolution is partly based on additional power (electricity), and wherever agriculture has prospered, new small-scale and cottage industries have sprung up.

In irrigation Maharashtra lags behind some other states. But its power consumption is high. If there were enough water to match this power, Maharashtra's affluence would be assured.

What applies to Maharashtra applies to all India?

The Green Revolution is not to be regarded as merely filling our bellies—though that is of primary importance. When it spreads to all India, it will create all-round prosperity.

People in India have experienced many spells of scarcity. They have learned lessons the hard way. The farmer is more alert today and the government actively helps him. With the spread of literacy, modern techniques will gain increasing currency. I am confident that the farmer will deliver bread to himself and to his fellow man.

---

india on the march

Acharya Vinoba Bhave

People often ask, what does the Bhoodan Movement mean?

Bhoodan actually means "land-gift." Land is a gift of God, like light and air. No one can—or should—own it. Wherever I walk through India, I ask rich landowners to share some of their land with the poor.

Is it correct to interpret Bhoodan as a campaign to collect and redistribute land?

Bhoodan is much more than just collecting and redistributing land. Ultimately the giving and receiving of land must be a dedication of one's all for the well-being of all. Were it not a moral reawakening, Bhoodan would be doomed to failure. Where there is love, where neighborliness is practiced, the sharing of land will be spontaneous.

What is the basic aim of Bhoodan?

Basically, to bring about a threefold revolution: a spiritual change in people's hearts; a physical change in improving their lives; and a change in the social structure—the welfare of all people. Bhoodan is not an end in itself but a beginning toward solving India's desperate agrarian problems and the formation of a casteless society based on brotherhood.

What is the role of the missionary in India today?

Unfortunately, the missionary in the past came to proselytize. Don't worry. Christ can take care of himself. Too many missionaries have served with ulterior motives. Today, the missionary should serve with his life, and the people will receive his message. Wherever he is, whatever his work, his greatest contribution is love.

Is money sent from America to India detrimental or beneficial?

Financial aid given in love is beneficial. We don't mind financial aid as long as there are no invisible strings attached. However, if aid is given with ulterior motives, it is detrimental.

Can Christians participate in the Bhoodan movement?

All can have a part in sharing. Surely you know how it is easier for a camel to pass through the eye of a needle than for a rich man to enter the Kingdom of God.

Cooperation means that if our religion is genuine, then our witness in the villages and on the roadside will be for the spiritual welfare of all people.

Acharya Vinoba Bhave is founder of the Bhoodan Land-Gift Movement.

HOPE THROUGH EDUCATION

revolution in education

Chandran Devanesen

In what ways is Madras Christian College distinctively Christian?

Madras Christian College has always been a pioneer in higher education in South India. The tradition goes back to the founder, Dr. William Miller, who established the first student dormitories at a time when most people thought this would be impossible, owing to the caste system. Many patterns of collegiate life now followed in South India were established by this college from the 1860s onwards so that "Christian College" has become a familiar household name in South India. The college has a tradition for experimentation.

Our directives in education point toward practical needs. In this period of our history, we feel that education becomes a luxury if it is not related to the needs of India. Many staff members have become acquainted with new concepts of development. We believe that the college can be an agency of development at this time, reaching out and helping surrounding villages to develop their economic strength. This requires not only concentrating on economic aspects but interpreting development in terms of the all-round growth of people in the area. To assist this program a number of experiments have been started; a higher elementary school for 800 children has transformed one village.

One of the young men from that village has graduated with an M.A. degree from this college. And one of the girls is now a medical student, so that the village has new leadership which has brought electricity, water, a reading room. In other words, this new sense of pride has created a different atmosphere in that village. The college is also experimenting with medical programs in surrounding villages. The Student Christian Movement runs a dispensary program. From this at least two outstanding leprologists have come, which shows the value of getting students interested in a problem while they are still in college.

Students have also been experimenting in liturgy; one of the changes is greater participation of students in forms of worship.

Dr. Devanesen is Principal of Madras Christian College, Madras.

Worship led by students has become a fresh innovative experience.

The college is also experimenting in a Family Life Institute. When our Child Welfare and Maternity Center is built, we hope to contact women of seven villages in this area through staff wives and willing students.

Will this include family planning?

Yes, but not just family planning. The program will start with dietetics, nutrition and child care. Perhaps we'll give them small industries like basket-weaving, sewing and then lead into family planning. We do not want to plunge straightway into family planning. First we must get a program established which gives the women confidence. They must be willing to trust us on this issue.

Another experiment is the establishment of a farm on our campus. We have a 100-acre farm with dairy, poultry, piggery and agricultural units run by our students and staff.

All this has been assisted by the fact that the minister of education has introduced the National Service Corps. Universities are steadily enrolling students in the National Service Corps. We have 200 students who are interested in various kinds of social work, including looking after 12 blind students.

Students also help pave village roads. In this period of our country's history, we want to get away from a textbook, information-absorbing type of education to a problem-solving field work type. In this way the student is pushed into trying to solve small problems so that he may then get involved in India's larger problems.

To what extent is the government backing colleges in this development program?

The major backing comes from the University Grants Commission. In the past two decades, it has not been missionary societies that have given us our major grants for development. I am not saying this in any critical way; I am only saying it is a good thing that our own Central Government of India has given substantial grants, and with these grants this college, for example, has passed from an undergraduate to a post-graduate institution with facilities for research. We receive these grants from the Central Government, the Council for Industrial and Scientific Research and also from industrial concerns.

Students are provided funds to travel throughout the Madras State (they are not confined to our district), testing public opinion. We must involve students in practical situations so that what they learn from textbooks confronts them as reality. Then the whole texture of Indian education can change so that students begin to apply their minds in practical ways to solutions instead of just thinking that they have to acquire a certain quantum of knowledge in order to pass an examination.

Can colleges provide adequate education for so many people?

People are hungry for education, and in a growing democratic society like ours, you can't deny education to the people. Expansion is not too rapid. The answer is to diversify education far more so that more professionals get more training and the humbler trades are dignified, as in the United States, by giving students diplomas and certificates. India cannot ignore the problem of numbers. We've got to deal with numbers but struggle to give a certain qualitative value also. It is a challenging struggle.

The block in Indian education is in perpetuating the London model, inherited from the nineteenth century. If there were more freedom to establish other patterns of higher education as in the United States or in Japan, for example, then India could break away from this outmoded London model of mother university with a number of satellite colleges all around it. Autonomous colleges would not break up the existing system but would show that within each university system there is sufficient field for experiment in courses, examinations and fresh methods of teaching. It could give much wider scope for pioneering and experimenting than is the case right now.

Do you face the revolutionary kind of ferment prevalent in American campus life?

Yes; instead of taking the revolution in education for granted professors must have an interest in seriously studying student problems. Only by a serious attempt to understand student unrest and what young people are passing through can we come to a meaningful relationship with them. For instance, we had a serious study of the reading habits of our students. We have also set up a counseling center where students can discuss their problems frankly. Students are referred to the center when they obviously need counseling or psychiatric treatment. When they need psychiatric treatment, they are sent to an expert.

But apart from serious cases, many students are baffled and bewildered by changes sweeping over them. We have the problem

of students who want to go modern, and students who are still very traditional. It exists on every Indian campus, but the conflict is deepening and sharpening. With girls, for example, the conflict is even more visible because it shows itself in dress. Some Indian girls want to wear miniskirts and bell-bottom trousers, instead of saris. "Why shouldn't we have the freedom to express ourselves the way we want?" they ask. And among men students also, some want a greater degree of permissiveness and togetherness. Certainly, as an educator, I have a good deal of sympathy with this. We started a Student Center where men and women students can mix, have coffee together and so on. But curiously, the Student Center comes under critical attack from traditional students.

*My hope lies
in the youth
of the country.*
   —*M. K. Gandhi*

India is passing through a transitional stage where certain students want greater freedom in relationships with the other sex, whereas other students are not quite sure it is right. Therefore, an educator has to be extremely wise in trying to control the pace of change in his institution, so he doesn't go too far ahead, while at the same time he must not be so stuck in the mud that he doesn't move at all. We are at a very interesting stage of the boy-girl relationship in India. In my institution plenty of campus romances have ended in satisfactory marriages between students, and even between staff and students.

Thus, the caste system also is changing through education. But there is a tendency on the part of the upper-crust caste to resist change. No one likes to see himself dispossessed of prestige or power, and this reflects itself even among certain segments of the student body.

Is there protest against institutionalization?

There is a growing protest against the bureaucracy and the impersonality of educational structures. This college attempts to anticipate revolt by conceding students the right to sit on various college committees, to make representation to the College Board of Review and have their own Student Council constitution.

Students now play a specific role in influencing college policies, including financial decisions. This is absolutely right. After all, students are in the vast majority. Whatever we try to do is for them. To cut them off from discussion of higher policy, whether academic or administrative, is unrealistic. The biggest change in educational thinking in India is the sudden realization that students are an important part of the universities. This is a move in the right direction. Madras Christian College has not fully succeeded, but student leadership is encouraged to be vocal and critical through their Student Council and their campus magazine, so that there is feedback.

What are some blocks in implementing change?

The biggest block in the Indian system of education is the British structure which governs us. Every college is part of some university system. But it's no use blaming the system. Even within the defects and limitations of the system, individual colleges have scope to experiment. We must be determined to move college education up to the point where it becomes scholarly and dares to experiment. Only then can a dent be made in the total educational system.

We've talked about the students having a say in policy. On the other hand, this is rather hard for some faculty members to take because they have not had a voice in policy. Yet students are demanding a say and getting it.

How would you summarize these aspects of campus unrest?

To sum it up, what we need is more experimentation so that there may be a breakthrough in the democratic structuring of all our educational institutions. Everybody involved in education must feel they belong, have a sense of participation and some share in policy-making and decisions. A person must feel he is wanted and part of the educational system if his contribution is to be meaningful.

We need dedicated teachers who are not only brilliant, but men and women who have character and concern. And such dedication can be engendered in schools like Madras Christian College. This, to answer your original question, is one of the basic distinctions of a Christian college.

---

campus unrest

Deepak Vohra

Would you say something about yourself and your background?

At present I am reading for a master's degree in English from St. Stephen's College, Delhi. I happen to be president of the student senate. The college is part of the University of Delhi complex. The degrees we earn are presented by the University of Delhi where over 75,000 students matriculate. The university is coeducational with about 45,000 girls and about 30,000 boys.

What are the responsibilities of a student senate president?

I suppose you'd first like to know something about the problems I have faced as president. Most, of course, are internal. I have faced problems every president faces—a multiplicity of allegations, meddling with funds, etc. But a more serious threat which faces not only our college but the entire university is what is known today throughout India as the Naxalite problem.

It started in a small village called Naxalbari in West Bengal, near Calcutta. In 1965 there was an armed peasant uprising led by a man called Kanu Sanyal. After this, there has been the growth of a cult of violence which derives its name from Naxalbari, known as Naxalism. Naxalites openly admit their allegiance to Red China. They believe in violence as a means of effecting social change and are in favor of demolishing the establishment not from within but outwardly by quick unexpected blows. One of their methods is to get a foothold in the most prominent educational institution in that area, destroy it, get wide publicity for their actions and create general consternation.

Deepak Vohra is President of the Student Senate, St. Stephen's College, Delhi.

In Calcutta, Naxalites began with the leading college there, Presidency College, which is being closed because of regular clashes between Naxalites and anti-Naxalites, bombing attacks, murders, looting, arson and widespread violence. In St. Stephen's College, ever since I became president, it seems to have acquired a fresh spurt—not that my being president had anything to do with it. It began with slogans appearing on the college walls.

A number of students from this college had abandoned their studies and gone underground to work for the underprivileged in the country; but of course, they joined the revolution, the Naxalite movement.

Slogans by Naxalites appeared, expressing their solidarity with comrades who had gone underground and calling upon others to do the same. Gradually they became more open, with various aspects of their ideology painted on college walls—slogans like "China's Chairman Is Our Chairman," "Long Live the People's War," "The People's Liberation Army Has Set Out," "You Fight Your Ways, We Fight Our Own," "We Fight Only When We Are Sure We Can Win," and quotations from Mao. The Naxalite movement has really been described as China's extended revolution here in India. Naxalites openly acknowledge violence and force as means of building a new society.

An unfortunate incident occurred recently. As president of the student body, I had to stop this sloganeering on college walls. We had a general meeting where slogan writing on college walls was condemned by three-quarters of the students present. We would condemn slogan writing even if Americans or Russians were doing it.

In retaliation, seven students came to my room in the dorm and assaulted me. I was in the hospital for some time and have just recovered. Thank God, they didn't injure me seriously, but they threatened to kill me if I continue to oppose them. They want me to quit.

Will you resign?

No. One of the fundamental tactics is to intimidate you, to create panic. If you really get scared, then they have won a great tactical victory. No sensible student in India will deny that the existing social system must be changed. For example, in the tea gardens in Calcutta, the ordinary worker is getting about twenty-five cents a day. Now do you really think a man earning twenty-five cents

a day can support a family of five or six? And when these people have sought to ameliorate these conditions through constitutional means, the few capitalists who control the government have clamped down with a firm hand. So they have very genuine, cogent grievances against the social system, which affords no opportunity for betterment to the underprivileged. I sympathize with them. But we feel that violence is not the answer. We want to change the present system. We do not want to destroy it because if we destroy it, we must build something after we succeed in demolishing the present one. This is what the Naxalites fail to realize. After they demolish the present structure, they have no really suitable alternative. And as such the movement cannot succeed. Students throughout the university are now very conscious of this warlike threat.

The Naxalite movement, which has about a thousand members at this university, spreads its tentacles throughout India seeking to stir up unrest on the campus.

The West basically considers Indians as a people of peace. What do Indian students think about the Vietnam war?

I'll give a representative opinion because we recently had a seminar in Delhi University. The topic was "Yankee Get Out of Vietnam." There were speakers both for and against the motion. In general, students here feel that American involvement in Vietnam is an impediment to a peaceful settlement in the area. They feel, first, that it was wrong for America to get involved at all. But now that America is involved, they must look as soon as they can for an honorable settlement. I assure you that a very large section of students here are not fanatical Maoists or pure Moscow types who say, "Yankee go home! And then we'll have a settlement." We realize that since America has continued fighting for such a long time, there must be a settlement which is not a detriment to either side. This is absolutely essential, not only in the interests of Vietnam but in the interests of world peace. Many of our generation sincerely believe this.

Is there a generation gap in India?

The generation gap has existed always. Today perhaps it tends to be more accentuated. Other than the Naxalite culture, there are two dominant cultures in India today. One might be described as the hippie culture, which is definitely anti-older generation. There is also an apathetic culture, which is not so much anti-older generation. But I don't think the generation gap as such exists in India to the degree that it does in the United States. I mean, we don't go around beating up old professors and locking them in their offices. We don't abuse our parents. We still have some respect. After all, respect and obedience to elders has been a fundamental tenet of Indian culture.

Is there a drug problem in India?

Yes, drug addiction is on the increase among students. It really hurts me whenever I see this mass of youngsters ruining themselves on LSD, heroin and marijuana. We hope that we can halt the movement.

Is the church doing anything to help in the drug problem?

Well, except for a few innocuous sermons from the pulpit, there's nothing much it can do. The Indian church has always been giving innocuous sermons—but seldom doing anything concrete. As a Hindu, I get the feeling that the church wants to help but does not know how.

Our college professes its education to be based on the life and teachings of Jesus Christ. I've gone to a missionary school also so I have very close contacts with the Christian church although I'm a Hindu. I feel that the church in its present form, despite its internal dissensions, despite its splintered denominations—Methodists, Calvinists, Anglicans, Puritans, Quakers, Presbyterians—the whole list of them who compete in outdoing one another in goodness—can play a very useful role in India.

The Christian church has something to offer which can be a very effective substitute for drugs. You see, ultimately what do these drug addicts want? Reality. Their drugs are a quest for reality. And the Christian church through its teachings, if propagated in a more dynamic form, can present effective methods, tried truths in this quest for reality. Yes, the Christian church has a much more important, active role to play than it is doing now. Of course, we have had some dynamic preachers at Delhi University who I have seen sway audiences of five thousand or more, keeping them spellbound. We need people like this who can propagate with zeal, with enthusiasm, the fundamental ideals of the Christian religion and point out how the Christian church in a modern scientific world can show an answer to world peace, and to man's ultimate striving for inner peace. This, I am convinced, is the greatest challenge facing the Christian church.

india's cultural ambassador to the west

Ravi Shankar

You have often been called India's cultural ambassador to the West. Do you feel Indian music has provided a bridge for better understanding between East and West?

Well, to be regarded a cultural ambassador between India and the West is indeed a compliment. But actually that is not for me to say. That is for the West to say.

I have tried to provide a bridge leading to better understanding between India and the West. To help accomplish this, I have been sincere in my art and cause. After long training, I have worked for about twenty years to explain and bring Indian music —particularly our classical music—to the West. I am gratified to see many changes occurring. Indian music was, when I first played before American audiences, considered some delicate, ancient museum piece. Very few people from the West understood or appreciated our music. Now, not only I but many other Indian concert musicians are touring America playing before large audiences. The door to this style of classical music is wide open. Indian music is now accepted as a serious form. It is no longer considered merely exotic—exciting for-a-little-while.

Western audiences have been unfamiliar with the art form of the sitar, a gourd-like instrument with nineteen sympathetic strings of which six are plucked to provide melody and thirteen are left free to provide resonance. In playing the ancient ragas, which can be traced back 2,000 years, there are no restrictions except for rhythm and key. The music is 95 percent improvisation and never can be played the same way, depending on the artist's mood. The artist has to develop a psychological buildup. For the raga is an artist's flight of fancy and an unappreciative audience—applauding, for example, or clicking and flashing cameras—can destroy the performance and mood the artist tries to create. Music is a window, a way of sharing. In India this music, like art, is an offering born in the temple.

Ravi Shankar, the internationally famous sitarist, is from Bengal.

CULTURE–
A WAY OF
SHARING

Music fills the infinite between two souls.
                                        —R. Tagore

Do you feel you have to make compromises in your performances before the musically uneducated public to make your music accepted?

No. I compromise nothing except the duration. This is my only compromise—the shortening of the lengthy ragas. In India when I play to regular listeners, who are familiar with our complex Indian forms of music, at times (not every performance) I really let myself go and there is no limitation of time. But in the West with union restrictions and so forth, people simply are not accustomed to sitting in one place so long.

In new places I try to restrict a performance to about two and a half hours. But where I have played previously, I do not necessarily limit the time. For instance, I played recently in Carnegie Hall for four and a half hours before an appreciative audience. Similarly, in San Francisco and Los Angeles I do not have to consider time; wherever people are accustomed to this art form and accept it, I do not have to make concessions in how long I play.

It's no use forcing people to accept the complexities and subtleties of Indian rhythms in one evening. Indian music at times is so intense it hurts. Many people—even Indians—have the wrong conception that unless ragas are played for at least two hours it is not pure classical music. That is not true. Our great Indian masters have performed on radio. They have made records—some of our finest are only three minutes. But the music is exquisite. That is the beauty of our Indian music. The secret is not how long you can make it. Before I begin to play before an audience, I try to ease the transition by explaining Indian music.

How do you account for the popularity of your music among youth in particular?

Listen to it and you know. All this did not happen in one day. It took time—lots of time. For over twenty years I have been coming to play in the West, and each time crowds have been growing. Between 1966-69 Indian music became almost a fad to many people. Because rock-and-roll players like the Beatles and the Rolling Stones used the sitar, it became a kind of fashion. People associated Indian music with this type of rock music. Americans started going to gurus to learn how to play the sitar, and people used to ask me how George Harrison was learning. People did not really come for Indian music itself but simply because it was a fad. But in spite of this, many people, after seriously listening to our music, liked it on its own merit. Basically, the beauty of our music outlasts fads because of the nature of improvisation. Thus our music is always fresh—always new—and the excitement the artist feels while performing is also felt by the audience.

It gives me great pleasure to see people without any background in Indian music appreciating it. But I do not play rock or primitive music. While I do not reject this form, I have nothing to do with rock-raga. Actually, the worlds of jazz, folk and electronic music have been influenced by our Indian music because they found something they didn't already have. But western music hasn't influenced me. We have not had to borrow from other cultures because our music grows within itself.

It is very difficult to try to explain the metrical design of ancient ragas. These include scientific classifications which are very technical. These combinations of flat and sharp notes are described in our ancient scriptures and theory of music books. Apart from all this, suffice it to say that the ragas have been for many, many centuries associations of ideas for Indians who are used to our music.

For many people—youth in particular—this ancient art form is accepted as a new experience.

indian art is like that

M. S. Randhawa

It is said that Indian art is colored by history, tradition, religious teaching. For over four thousand years India has suffered invasion and conquest, violence, hunger, poverty. Is this reflected in Indian art?

Indian art is not like that, although ancient history and traditions are reflected in art as well as in ancient literature of this country. Sculptures of 200 B.C. reflect not only style of dress but religious practices often related to fertility cults. There is a legend that the Buddha was born under an asoka tree; so these became known as fertility trees. Women who wanted children used to pray to these trees for the birth of a boy because sons are favored in India. This tree worship led to the development of a very beautiful type of sculpture.

India has an ancient civilization as old as 2500 B.C. Ours was a flourishing civilization. Then Buddhism came, about 500 B.C., when India was the most civilized country in the world. And from that time to about A.D. 1100 her art spread to Central Asia, Ceylon, Indochina, Java, Sumatra, China and other parts of the Orient.

India maintained this cultural lead in many ways, having a high standard of living. India regarded the Greeks as equals, but the

Dr. Randhawa is Vice Chancellor, Punjab Agricultural University, Ludhiana.

rest of the world as barbarians. So this problem of hunger and poverty is recent and developed with the growth of population.

At one time India was one of the most affluent nations in the world and during that period produced her best art and literature. How lovely are some of these paintings, the finest in the world! They reflect not hunger, not poverty, but carefreeness, ease and joy. Her great paintings of Ajanta reflect feelings of compassion, which you see in faces. Paintings on paper developed in India in the thirteenth century. In the sixteenth century Akbar collected all the skilled artists in India along with master painters from Persia and patronized them. Thus began the Moghul school of painting, truly Indian in spirit.

Most Indian art, particularly Kangra painting, deals with the theme of human love—love of man and woman. This art captures the various moods of men and women. One example is a painting of a lady standing near the door of her house waiting for her lover. In our own country, you must have seen women standing in the doors saying good-bye to their men when they are leaving or welcoming them when they are expected back. This is a universal feeling and a universal theme. That's why paintings which show the feelings of men and women are beautiful. Apart from that, these artists used very fine brushes and lovely colors; they glow like jewels even after 250 years; and it's beautiful, inspirational art, which gives great happiness when one is distressed or weary. Such art takes you to a romantic, faraway world. That's what authentic art can do.

Is contemporary painting done similarly, or is there a change in art?

There is a very big change. These paintings which I mentioned are an ancient art—long lost. One painting would take many months to complete; the colors were carefully ground. Artists used mineral colors and this was a work of great patience, slowly grinding the colors. Such painting could be done only in areas where artists were supported by rich patrons, enabling them to be carefree so that they could concentrate on their work. So this art could only develop under feudal patronage and when feudalism vanished, the artists also vanished.

Whom do you consider the outstanding contemporary artists?

Of the present artists in India, I consider Satish Gujral of New Delhi because he shows in his paintings the sufferings of the Punjab people after Partition in 1947 when refugees fled to India. Also,

I do not want my house to be walled on all sides and my windows stuffed. I want the cultures of all the lands to be blown about my house as freely as possible. But I refuse to be blown off my feet by any.
—M. K. Gandhi

Paul Raj, who lives in Madras, sensitively captures the struggle of South Indians.

---

the struggle
of journalism in india

Khushwant Singh

What changes have taken place in journalism in India?

Changes occurring in India in particular are the enormous increase in publication circulation of Indian news in fourteen different Indian languages, including English. These publications don't begin to touch India's population. Papers are restricted in their circulation to cities, and to literate people who total less than 30 percent even to this day.

Most mass communication is done through All India Radio, a government monopoly. The government has refused, despite recommendations, to set up a corporation like the BBC [British Broadcasting Corporation] in England. We can safely say that 70 percent of the population is now reached by All India Radio, and less than 10 percent of the urban population is reached by newspapers.

The percentage of people who read English in India is about 1 percent, but they are the people in power. To this day, people who matter are English speaking, and therefore to edit an English journal such as a daily or weekly paper is of considerable importance.

The Illustrated Weekly of India by American standards has a modest circulation of 160,000 copies. Research shows that each copy is read by more than 27 people, so we actually have a circulation readership of over 4 million, and that is very satisfying, despite the fact that literacy increases at a very slow pace. This is partly due to shortage of paper; it's difficult to reach villagers to increase our literacy rate.

What is the literacy rate?

The government claims a little over 30 percent of the population is literate. But I would say it is between 20 and 25 percent.

Khushwant Singh is Editor of The Illustrated Weekly of India, *Bombay.*

> *Not all writers can break into journalism*
> *today the way Mahatma Gandhi did. He had*
> *not seen a newspaper until he went to Lon-*
> *don at the age of 18. Yet he became not*
> *only a prince among journalists, but cre-*
> *ated more weekly papers than any other*
> *single person in journalistic history. He*
> *had no journalistic training of any kind.*
> *His writing was literature in a hurry—for*
> *he unpacked his heart in it.*
>
> *—A. Noble Rajamani,*
> *Freelance Writer*

And is TV still in the distant future?

Not such a distant future. New Delhi has television and uses it advantageously on occasions such as Republic Day. However, it is a very small circuit covering a few square miles.

Television will have an important role for propaganda purposes. Pakistan, for example, beams its propaganda to India and there are receiver sets all along our frontier posts and villages. Even towns and villages have TV picking up Radio Pakistan, so India countermands it by setting up a station in the Kashmir Valley. Bombay will have TV within the next five years. There will be an enormous communication spurt. Television factories are being set up now. TV will in turn improve the prospects of freelance writers.

What are the prospects of a freelance writer in India?

It depends. If he can break into the foreign market as well, let's say the American market, then he is well off because a dollar goes a long way. If he is restricted to papers in India, he has a hard struggle. The English papers pay more than any others; for instance, mine would pay up to $30 an article, which is modest. But if an Indian can sell two articles a month to a paper like *The Illustrated Weekly of India,* he can live on $60 a month. The Indian papers, even Hindi, which are the next largest, pay very little. A writer may be paid $4 for an article. One can't hope to make a living in freelance journalism unless he has considerable backing and experience and has been commissioned or works with a syndicate. Then he can manage.

Does the government control the press?

I believe the government is controlling the press, but what is important is that inroads are being made. An editor or a journalist can't be sacked today; once a man is hired by a newspaper he is there for a long time and if he has the will and the integrity he can put his views across to the masses.

There are three aspects to freedom of the press, three things which make a paper: 1) newsprint, 2) printing machinery and 3) news agencies. In India, all three are under government control. The biggest paper producing plants are government controlled, so if the government wants to make editors conform, it just reduces the amount of available paper. Printing presses which are not manufactured in India can only be imported under licenses. If government doesn't like what you print, it stops licenses. Another factor is that the government is the single largest advertiser in the country, and most papers live by advertising.

The government controls many holdings. When any paper is critical of the government, suddenly the advertising is withdrawn. I know several specific cases. The prestigious *Statesman* of Calcutta ran a candid article critical of the government's stand in Kashmir. Suddenly, its advertising was shrugged off and the publishers had to retract the article. In recent months we have had two examples: one of my own chain of papers, the *Times of India*, was critical of government policy. Advertising was withdrawn. But a smaller paper, the *Tribune* of Chandigarh, went afoul of the government and the chief minister had the audacity to actually stop the entry of the *Tribune* into the state until the rest of the press created a stink against him. So we have to fight the government at district, state and central levels. We have to continue to fight against the government to maintain open and honest communication.

We followed with much interest your issues on a series of different religions, including "Why I Am a Christian" and "How Christmas Is Celebrated by Different Churches." Is there any value in discussing the pluralism of religions in India?

I believe in religious tradition as long as it gives a sense of identity or belonging; that is why I am a Sikh.

There is enormous interest in religions in the world, and certainly in India, which has a variety of them. But Indians know so little about the other person's religion. This country is rich with different sects and communities with fascinating customs, rites and class distinctions. Prejudices arise from ignorance, and the first time I started highlighting the different customs, manners, traditions, readers began learning not only about themselves but about their neighbors. People have often said that I am making them conscious of their community differences. But that is not true. As a matter of fact, people have been fascinated to know that other people have similar or different customs and religious beliefs, and so interest has grown.

My primary interest is not the revival of religion but the revival of tradition, knowledge and sense of belonging. It's a sort of "Let a thousand flowers bloom." We are all different and yet we are all the same. We are one people with different kinds of fragrances and colors.

What is the church doing for India and her people?

It's a risk for a non-Christian journal to objectively present the work of the church. India owes a great deal to the Christian church in the way of development, relief work, education, hospitals. I am a great admirer of the missionary effort in this country. There is, unfortunately, a revival of Hinduism. Eighty-five percent of the people in the country are Hindus. They have been ruled by the British and Muslims in turn. For the first time, they have come into their own, so there is this resurgence of aggressive Hinduism. They won't have any more of Christian missionary work, so they have legislation in several states against conversion. I don't stand for it; I think it is wrong. The Indian Christian is taking it lying down. He is almost shamefaced about being a Christian. He is made to feel that being Christian is not being Hindu and therefore not being a good enough Indian. That doesn't apply to the Syrian Christian church, which is as old as some sects of Hinduism in this country; but it does apply to Protestant churches of northern India, whose converts keep their Hindu names. It is a great trial for Christianity, and I hope that Christianity will come out on top.

RELIGIONS OF THE INDIAN SOIL

salute to the foreign missionary

Khushwant Singh

What are your candid feelings toward foreign missionaries?
Let me begin with this simple incident.

Some years ago I got to know a girl working in the British High Commission. She was barely thirty when she became a first secretary. She was a very unusual person; she had won scholarships through school and college, got a first in her Cambridge Tripos and topped the list in the Foreign Service examination. It was obvious that she had a bright future as a diplomat. Unlike most foreigners, she did not mix with her own countrymen but with Indians; the only English people I saw in her spacious bungalow were unkempt lads unable to afford hotels or servicemen of lower ranks.

Once she happened to go for a holiday to Nepal. On her way back to Katmandu her plane had to make an emergency landing at Pokhra. Pokhra had no hotel so she had to spend a night at a leper sanatorium run by missionaries. When she returned to Delhi, I could sense something had happened to her. She often brought up the leprosarium in her talk.

A few days later, two Pokhra missionaries came to spend their first holiday in many years with her in Delhi. There was something delightfully childish in the way they went round, pressing electric switches to see the miracle of light and pulling chains to

Khushwant Singh is Editor of The Illustrated Weekly of India, *Bombay.*

Based on an article in *The Illustrated Weekly of India,* Jan. 4, 1970. Used by permission.

watch water cascade into the lavatory basin. Some time after the departure of the guests, this girl gave up her job.

"There's more to life than drinking duty-free liquor at diplomatic receptions," she told me laconically.

Two years later I met her in England. She was living in a single-bedroom apartment. She earned a very modest salary and certainly could not afford to swill liquor of any kind. But she bubbled with life. The sense of euphoria her work gave her was contagious. And her work was looking after drunks, delinquents, orphans, the aged and the sick. She was (and is) a living proof

*Human devel-
opment is
based upon
love and
social recon-
struction.
—Vinoba
Bhave*

that there is more to life than getting a big salary, living in comfort, wielding power and distributing patronage.

The girl is not *Christian* in the conventional sense of the term. She does not go to church or even pray at home. She is like many other good people who do not find it necessary to believe in institutionalized religion. It is, however, strange that Christian ethos more than anything else produces the type dedicated to the ideal of *nishkāma karma* [doing your duties without attachment]. In the 1947 civil strife, the only band of people I saw working among the warring communities in India as well as in Pakistan were

Christian Quakers. Similarly, in the famines in Bihar the really organized band of voluntary workers were Christians (Ramakrishna Mission was the only other group). Personally, I see nothing wrong in gaining converts by good acts but those who are irked by it should know that the vast majority of Christians engaged in community service today have little or no interest in evangelism.

I praise foreign missionaries because they initiated and are even today the driving force behind most organized Christian endeavor.

Consider how many Hindus, Muslims and Sikhs were born in Christian maternity homes, educated in Christian schools and colleges and treated in Christian hospitals.

Consider the sacrifices made by men and women who abandon the comforts and security of life in Europe and America to run these maternity homes, schools, colleges and hospitals.

Consider what we owe to these people who work among our poorest Harijans [outcastes], orphans, abandoned women and children, the blind and the handicapped.

And then consider the ingratitude of those who, without any proof whatsoever, accuse them of base motives of bribery to win adherents or serving foreign political interests. We give the generations of foreign missionaries who worked and gave their lives to serve India our grateful thanks.

---

missionary activity in a non-christian land

C. Rajagopalachari

What type of missionary workers are wanted in present day India?

Perhaps your question should be, should any missionary workers come at all to India?

My opinion is that it is not really possible on the grounds of revelation, or logic, or on the evidence of miracles to hold that among the religions known as Hinduism, Jainism, Buddhism, Islam and Christianity, any one is nearer the truth than any other.

C. Rajagopalachari is a former Governor-General of India.

I object to the exclusive claim for truth, if any, made on behalf of any one of these faiths.

If this point is accepted, the only justification for missionary work (which I understand is proselytization, whatever the means adopted), is expediency in the best sense of the term.

Is it good on the whole for men and women to change from one religion to another?

If people profess any religion to which they are born, which fosters and promotes right conduct and social cooperation, it is not desirable to make efforts for proselytization among them. Such efforts undermine their present faith, which is good enough for promoting right conduct and deterring them from sin, and tend to disturb family and social harmony.

Ardent believers have plenty of work to do among their own people to get them to follow the precepts of their faith.

I am wholly against making proselytization a calling for young men and women. No one should think of such work before he or she is mature and then not for a wage, either from an individual employer or an organization.

The work of healing or teaching or the like should not start from, or in any way be mixed up with, the motive of changing the faith of the persons under influence. Doctors and teachers should arrive or be sent for exclusively for the practice of the respective professions.

Why disturb other people's religions? That's an ancient evil. . . . Let people follow their own religion in a nonviolent and peaceful way.

Nehru once said, "Christianity is as old in India as Christianity itself. Christianity found its roots in India before it went to countries like England, Portugal and Spain. Christianity is as much a religion of the Indian soil as any other religion of India." Would you comment on that?

In a sense, it is true that New Testament Christianity is nearer to our Hindu religion than any other religion because Christianity is based on compassion and love. There is no difference between Christ and love among the educated in India today. So I say let a person discover for himself and choose the religion which helps him live a useful life.

One peculiarity of the Christian faith is that there is more emphasis on love and compassion than on anger and fear. But fear and anger also have their place if you are dealing with people who cannot otherwise be convinced. Therefore, the phrase "God-fearing" has come into existence. The phrase itself is a contradiction in terms. God is not a person whom we should fear; we should love him. All the same, I would be content with fearing God if it helps me to act properly—as we love our wives but also fear them. We fear their displeasure, don't we? We should not fear God, but we should fear his displeasure.

I have expressed my opinions frankly but with no want of respect for those who work on the basis of their own faith, and I hope I shall not be misunderstood.

Christianity is as old in India as Christianity itself. Christianity found its roots in India before it went to countries like England, Portugal and Spain. Christianity is as much a religion of the Indian soil as any other religion of India.

—Jawaharlal Nehru

yoga

K. M. Agarival

What is Indian yoga?

Yoga has been interpreted in many different terms. Yoga is the word which means our direct relation with the divine.

How can we find that relation?

Everyone has what we call psychic being, which is the direct representative of the divine in oneself. The divine is God. Christians call Christ the representative of God. That power is part of divine power. It is there in every human being, whether one knows it or not, because it is in the process of evolution. Strictly speaking, yoga means our psychic being, which is part of the divine. Yoga enables us to find *selfhood.*

How does one find oneself?

One finds oneself through meditation, introspection. When we are silent, we can concentrate on the psychic being, and try to bring that psychic being forward into relationship with the divine mind. In the initial stages, one has to sit quietly for some time. One has to keep a separate time for it. That is very necessary. By gradual practice the pyschic being awakens.

Can yoga be used in religious services such as the church?

Certainly yoga can be used in religious services. Religion is not an obstruction to yoga; rather, it helps.

We in the States look upon India as a country of peace, a country that helps perpetuate peace. Is anything being done to develop peace in the midst of revolutionary elements in India?

We believe in peace. Our very culture is based on peace. Hindus don't believe in killing. Humanity has to become one whole universal brotherhood. There was a time when nationalism flourished. People believed in nationalism, and they died for their nation, but not anymore. Universal brotherhood is necessary in this doctrine of life, the salvation of humanity. Nuclear weapons can destroy the entire universe in a few hours. This consciousness of brotherhood may be developed in man now through yoga. Many times during the day I pray for peace starting with me.

Dr. Agarival is Director of the Yoga Center, Lucknow.

Oh, God
I know you are
Lord of my being.
You control
all my motions
all my sentiments
all my sensations
all the movements of my life
each cell of my body
each drop of my blood.
I'm absolutely yours.
Tell me, what shall I do?
Whether you choose for me
life or death
happiness or sorrow
pleasure or suffering
all that comes to me from you will be welcome.
Each one of your gifts
will be always for me
a gift of honor.
Bring with it a supreme felicity
and peace.
Amen.

---

the importance of
christian participation

J. R. Chandran

What are some major tasks facing the Christian church in modern day India?

When we look at Indian national life today and ask what the role of Christians is, four tasks become very compelling.

The first is national integration, overcoming the divisiveness of communalism, regionalism, linguism, casteism, class conflict and other evils. In this context, how can the church be an effective servant of God for the good of the nation as long as it is itself so

Dr. Chandran is Principal of the Theological Seminary, Bangalore.

badly divided by denominationalism and other considerations? The second is the establishment of a just society free from inequalities and discriminations. In the context of religious and cultural pluralism, wide disparities in the sharing of wealth and the need to preserve freedom and liberty for all, only a secular democratic socialism can provide justice for all. This would place a responsibility upon all Christians to give active support to a political party which, in their judgment, is really committed to the establishment of a secular, democratic and socialistic society.

Thirdly, in order that Christians may play a meaningful role in national life, they need to be mobilized for political education of themselves as well as others. This is one of the main aims of Christian union in India. Political education can be imparted only through participation in specific political activities such as proper exercise of the franchise, organizing public opinion against social and economic evils in local, regional or national spheres and other political programs. It is also essential to cooperate with others in defining and formulating economic and social goals.

Fourthly, it is important that Christians' source of inspiration and power is their communion with Christ. Therefore, we should guard against the wrong type of secularization of people trying to live on their own human resources. The high standards of service and moral integrity which we badly need in public life today cannot be established merely through human programs. Without men whose dedication to service and moral integrity is witness to a higher loyalty, programs cannot achieve much. Christians can fulfill their calling to participate effectively with the rest of the Indian people in the struggle for a just and humane society only if they continue as disciples of Christ, whose mission is the renewal of humanity.

the crescent and the cross

Hasan Askari

What is the Muslim's contribution in India today?
Frankly, little. Being Muslim myself, I feel that the Muslim personality today in India is an inauthentic personality, partly due

to recent human events in India, namely the division of the country, and partly due to the Muslim's unpreparedness. There are many linguistic and cultural barriers. The general feeling of being threatened develops a fetish identity and hence incapacitates Muslims to grapple with political and religious problems. This feeling of insecurity is increasing, and Muslims are made to fall back upon a kind of debtor solution, both mentally and physically.

A cultural bridge between Hindus and Muslims is difficult but necessary. In the medieval ages in India a cultural bridge did exist. Perhaps there may be new hope in the seventies. There has been no cultural conflict—particularly in music. The great Muslim masters of Indian music, for example, were practically worshiped by their Hindu disciples. Then too, there is a resurgence of mysticism in both Islam and Hinduism. These are hopeful signs.

Are there signs of reformation in Islam?

The real challenge for the Muslim in India is primarily cultural and secondarily political. By *cultural challenge,* I mean a certain dichotomy in the Muslim mind. For more than seven hundred years they have been the masters of this part of the world. A sense of loss, both historical and psychological, was experienced when the country was divided. During the last two decades, Muslims in general have been unable to comprehend what this loss is. Sometimes they see it in economic terms, sometimes in political terms. What is really at the back of this sense of loss is the historical question of relationship between authority and faith. For the first time in the history of Muslim society, the Muslim in this particular subcontinent has been called upon to formulate a new relationship between authority and faith. Islam always took in the Middle East, North Africa and the Far East; Islam, being perfect, as the Muslim thinks it to be, obviously should develop historical roots proudly and fully and Islam should be a historical success as it was when it began.

Now the Muslim is unable to understand why a believer should lose his history. Why? What is the meaning of the sovereignty of God in relation to people suffering when they lose their former empire? Here he must acquire a new orientation of faith. Unfortunately he is not being helped by his Hindu neighbor because the Hindu in India also does not have experience comparable in

Professor Askari is a sociologist at Osmania University, Hyderabad.

history except in mythology. The Hindu, too, is on slippery ground in modern India because his orientation in time does not fit the demands of industrial, mechanical time which he is called upon to accept in the contemporary age. There is a certain inadequacy common to both: the Hindu is incapable of translating mythical into historical time; the Muslim is incapable of translating his loss of authority into spiritual gain.

Where are the Christians in this particular context?

I ask myself this question again and again. Both Muslims and Hindus are inarticulate in translating their respective spiritual traditions into contemporary historical life. Muslims need the Christian concept of God not only as sovereign but also suffering, not only the Lord of history, but also its "victim." Muslims in India need this particular concept of God in order to bridge the gap between faith and authority, between the crescent and the cross. There must be a recovery of faith.

why i am a christian

J. Victor Koilpillai

Why are you a Christian?

Christians have surrounded Jesus Christ with much theology and many abstractions, through which, however, shine the messages

J. Victor Koilpillai is Director of the Lucknow Publishing House and Editor of Indian Witness.

Based on an article in *The Illustrated Weekly of India,* Dec. 27, 1970. Used by permission.

and the call. Acceptance brings peace, not in some other world, but here and now. I find the Christian Gospel a constant challenge and an adequate resource for a fuller, more fruitful life. Christianity is essentially a way of life; being a Christian is only partly believing—it is mostly living.

The Christian faith, for instance, provides the foundation and the inspiration to my belief in democracy and my attempts to practice it. The message of the Bible is that man is created in the image of God, and Christ died for all men. This is the supreme assertion of the equality—the equal worth—of all men before God, and therefore of man before man.

Acceptance of this truth leads to or helps formulation of a social order in which the values of democracy could be realized, such as individual liberty, the right to rule ourselves, tolerance, equal rights and opportunities to all citizens. It helps me to recognize the common humanity in mankind and to accept fellow man as myself, overcoming the prejudices that arise from differences in color, culture and creed.

This is also the spiritual anchor of my belief in the brotherhood of man and hope for its realization, because it is rooted in God. Despite all signs to the contrary, I believe that the desire for brotherhood is latent in all men, and active in those who accept the fatherhood of God. I am conscious that not all Christians reflect this belief in practice.

How is the Christian way of life summed up?

The Christian way of life is summed up in Christ's great commandment, "Love the Lord your God with all your heart . . . . love your neighbor as yourself." Christ calls for obedience as a spontaneous expression of love for him. It was not given as a formula, but I find it a most adequate guide to a life of inward peace and personal fulfillment at the highest spiritual level.

Communion with God is a means of spiritual strength, the way to peace of mind, which the world seeks so much today. It is the result, not of an artificial mental exercise, but of a natural drawing together of the creature towards the creator in wonder, worship and love.

Prayer and meditation are not empty rituals, but actual communication with a very personal being, who is close, concerned and consoling. I would otherwise have no use for prayer. The sense of forgiveness, assurance, the tranquility that comes from such communion is the peace that restless modern man seeks. God is ready to be found if man would but seek him.

Love for God is not expressed in isolation from man; a social responsibility goes with it, for Christianity is not an other-worldly religion. It is intensely secular because the Christian life of love, peace and joy is lived now in this world. The second part of Christ's great commandment covers all aspects of social responsibility; concern for fellow man is the soundest basis on which can be built a society in which human welfare and social justice can be assured.

Complexities of modern life no doubt present difficulties in deciding the right way to ensure the maximum well-being of man in society. Christianity, however, is not mere idealistic goody-goodiness, oblivious of human weakness, especially the proneness of man towards sin. The presence of sin is recognized, but I find in Christ the assurance of man's ability to overcome sin, and the strength to do so. Above all, to those who repent and change, there is forgiveness; they must of course surrender themselves to Christ's guidance and resolve to lead a new life.

Does the new life in Christ entail suffering?

To return to the paradox of Christ's teaching—his injunction to love does not mean being good only to those who are nice to us; it is a call to love without counting the cost—to go the second mile, to give away one's coat besides the cloak, to turn the other cheek. It entails suffering certainly, but suffering for others. Such a way of life is the high spiritual destiny to which man is called by Christ.

It separates him more completely than anything else from other animals; in fact it makes him reflect the divine nature, the character of God revealed in Christ. It was exemplified in Christ's suffering and death. Such love, though sometimes causing physical suffering, produces a joy and inward peace that the world can neither give nor take away.

Love has been seen in the lives of men like St. Francis of Assisi, Sadhu Sundar Singh, Dr. Toyohiko Kagawa of Japan and countless ordinary people. The cross was the inspiration of Deenabandhu C. F. Andrews, Mahatma Gandhi, Martin Luther King, Jr., and others. They found joy in spending themselves for others.

Even in our daily life we can see that those who are active in the welfare of others are always more at peace with themselves and their neighbors, and possess such tranquility and cheerfulness as self-centered people never have.

Hence the declaration of Christ that "He who finds his life shall lose it, and he who loses his life for my sake will find it." In at least trying to attain to that level of living, I find the way to be at peace with the world and grow spiritually. Christ's call to love brings out the noblest in man and raises him above love of himself to his highest fulfillment as a member of a family and nation.

Therefore, I feel that I can justifiably claim that in Christ are to be found the answers to all of man's needs and the way to fulfillment of all his aspirations.

In the fellowship of the church to which I belong, I find the nourishment that results from a group of like-minded persons meeting together for worship, study and discussion. In the sharing of experiences and problems of Christian living in light of the Bible, and seeking help through corporate prayer, is spiritual strength for everyone.

What weaknesses confront the church?

An organization of human beings set in this world, the church is subject to many temptations and has several divisions, weaknesses and failings. But its calling and mission are divine, in fulfilling which, through the centuries, it has come a long way. It has to be continually renewed by the power and grace of God. I consider it a privilege to belong to it.

This is not a communal body with narrow interests, but a fellowship dedicated to proclaiming and demonstrating the love of God to all people. In the midst of conflicts and frustrations, the assurance of redemption in Christ is the beacon of hope which I follow in faith. Without such hope I would not be able to live today. Not only the individual, but the whole creation is seeking to be united with God, according to the prophetic writings in the Bible.

Repeatedly mankind is driven to seek God in some way after finding that a better world and a peaceful one cannot be built on mere knowledge and science. My hope is strengthened by the fact that Christ is not a figure of the past, one who spoke, suffered and died long ago.

Christ lives and is active in the hearts of people and the existence of nations ever since he began his work by the shores of Lake Galilee. To possess this faith and hope, and be brought up in it, is more than I shall want in this world.

ACKNOWLEDGMENTS

Special acknowledgment is due to Arthur Lall, former Ambassador from India to the United States a̶ ̶ ̶̶ore̶ ̶epresentative to the United Nations, for serving s̶ ̶ ̶̶ ̶̶nsultant, giving warm and wise suggestions in prepa̶ ̶ ̶̶n.

Particular gratitude is expresse̶ ̶ ̶̶ Barbara Harkins and Mrs. Marie Hoffmann for their a̶ ̶ ̶̶e in transcribing, typing and proofing these interviews.

Appreciation for permission to quote from publications in part or in whole is gratefully acknowledged to:

Khushwant Singh, Editor, *The Illustrated Weekly of India:*
> *Salute to the Foreign Missionary* by Khushwant Singh, January 4, 1970
> *Why I Am a Christian* by J. Victor Koilpillai, December 27, 1970
> *Three or Two or One or None* by Dr. S. N. Agarwala, February 7, 1971

Dr. S. Chandrasekhar, *Prevention Is Better Than Cure.* Central Family Planning Institute, New Delhi, India. 1970.